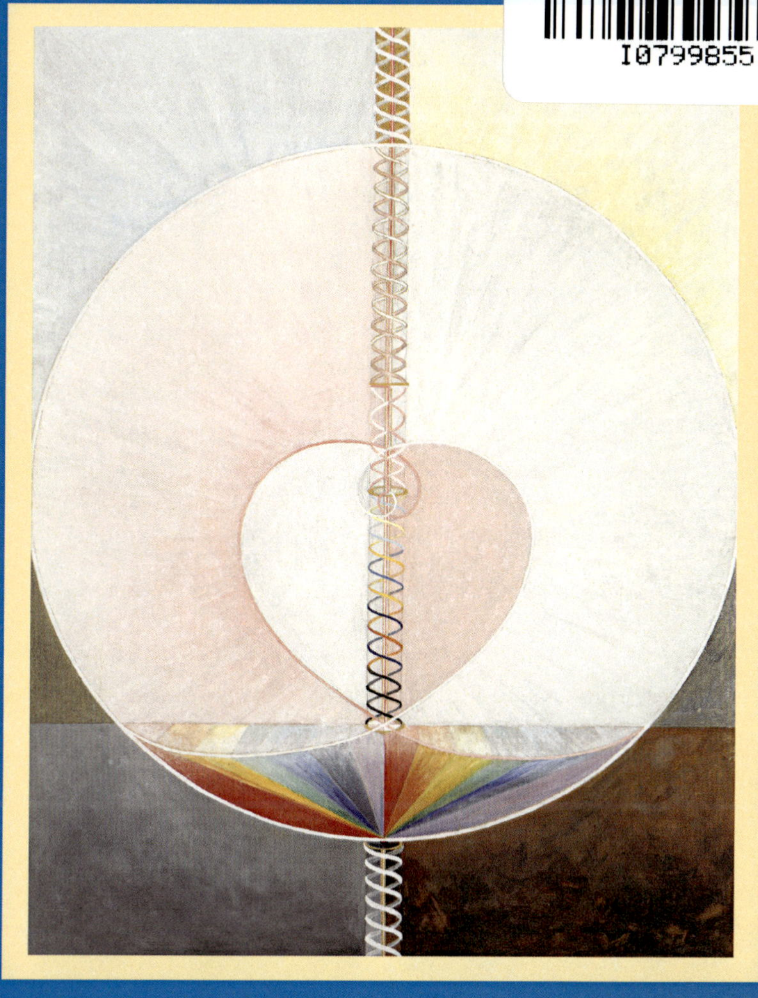

Hilma af Klint's Philosophy of Life

Johan af Klint

Edited and Afterword by Rachel Villari

STONE TOWER PRESS

Hilma af Klint's Philosophy of Life

Stone Tower Press
7 Ellen Rd.
Middletown, RI 02842
stonetowerpress.com

Printed in the United States of America

Cover art:

The figure on the front side of the cover is:
The UW Series, Group IX, *The Dove, No. 1.* 1915. HaK 173. 151.0 x 114.5 cm. Oil on canvas.

The figure on the back cover is:
The WUS/Seven-Pointed Star Series, Group V, *Seven-Pointed Star, No. 2.* 1908. HaK 49.
75.5 x 62.0 cm. Tempera and gouache.

ISBN: 979-8-9919831-4-3

Library of Congress Cataloging-in-Publication Data

Names: af Klint, Johan, 1939 – author. | Villari, Rachel, editor.

Title: Hilma af Klint´s Philosophy of Life/Johan af Klint; edited by Rachel Villari

Identifiers: 979-8-9919831-4-3 (paperback)

Subjects: LCSH: af Klint, Hilma, 1862–1944. | Painter-Sweden-Philosophy of Life, | Woman painters-Sweden-Philosophy of Life.

Formatted and designed by Amy Cole, JPL Design Solutions

Contents

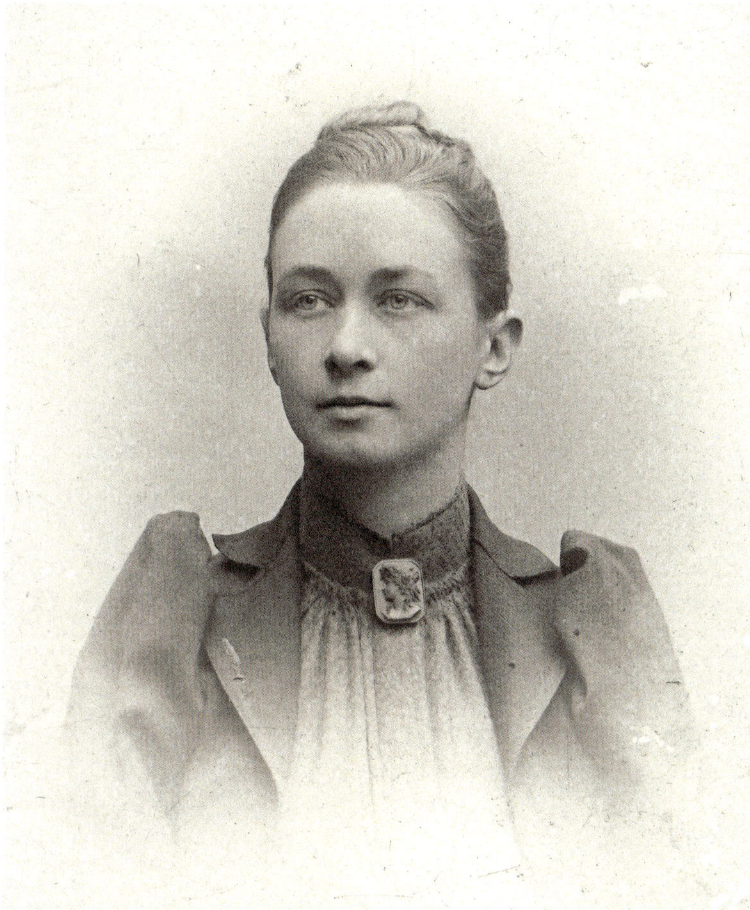

Figure 1. *Hilma af Klint, circa 1895*
Courtesy of The Hilma af Klint Foundation
Photo: Moderna Museet, Stockholm, Sweden

Introduction

Hilma af Klint, my grandfather's sister, entrusted her symbolic works, notebooks, and religious items—collectively known as her "Work"—to my father, Vice Admiral Erik af Klint.

In this article, we endeavor, on the one hand, to present a professional analysis of Hilma af Klint's philosophy of life, as well as, on the other hand, to present a suggested interpretation of the *spiritual message to humanity* included in her *Drawings to the Temple*. This latter aspect is only a well-documented suggestion for academic researchers to grasp and further develop.

Unfortunately, her non-figurative paintings have during the past decades come to be described merely as *art*—more specifically as *abstract art*. However, her works are *sacred* containing a *spiritual message to humanity* from higher dimensions.[1] In this article, we endeavor to return to Hilma af Klint's original definitions—e.g. the *Drawings to the Temple*.[2] To avoid

1 See also below under the sub-heading "*1. Hilma af Klint as a Renaissance Person*."

2 HaK 555, p. 14, 4 February 1906.

Furthermore, in order to prevent any misunderstanding, the word "Temple" is written with a capital "T," when reference is made to Hilma af Klint's desired Temple.

the word *art* in this article, her painted non-figurative works are categorized as *symbolic works.*[3]

This presentation will initially provide brief introductory comments to:

- Hilma af Klint as a person;
- Hilma af Klint's extraordinarily strong inspiration;
- The various phases in her symbolic works;
- Hilma af Klint's relationship to Rudolf Steiner;
- Her relationship to the Anthroposophical Society.

After these introductory comments, some views will be presented as:

- Hilma af Klint's Philosophy of Life and its reflections in her symbolic works; and
- The *spiritual message to humanity* inherent in the *Drawings to the Temple.*

Finally, we present the *Afterword* by Rachel Villari.

3 When Hilma af Klint and her Work were introduced to the public via various distinguished international art museums, the art historians unfortunately regarded her painted non-figurative works as mere *abstract art* and called them the *Paintings to the Temple.* They even argued whether she was the initiator of *abstract art.* However, the form of *abstract art* is to be found much earlier in tantric drawings, in motifs that adorn mosques, in numerous medieval European manuscripts, etc. In addition hereto, Georgiana Houghton, Annie Besant and Charles W. Leadbeater presented *abstract paintings* prior to Hilma af Klint in 1906.

Horowitz, 2024, p. 35.

However, Hilma af Klint painted primarily *spiritual* works, which included a *spiritual message to humanity* from higher dimensions. The works ought, therefore, primarily to be regarded as *sacred*—in the same manner as we regard Icons. Only on a *second-hand basis* should her paintings be regarded as non-figurative or *abstract* paintings. This is the reason why we, in this article, have returned to Hilma af Klint's own denomination—e.g. *Drawings to the Temple.* Consequently, her painted non-figurative works are called *symbolic works* in this article.

The Article

Hilma af Klint in a "Nutshell"

Hilma af Klint left behind more than 1,500 symbolic works, as well as 124 notebooks encompassing about 26,000 handwritten and typed pages, and some religious items. All of this, will be referred to as her Work.

The studies of the Work during the past few years have revealed that Hilma af Klint was a much more advanced and developed person, than was earlier believed. Consequently, one may now consider her as a:

Renaissance Person
Mystic
Prophet

Let us see what these statements may entail!

1. *Hilma af Klint as a Renaissance Person*

Hilma af Klint (1862–1944) was a Swedish artist, who is regarded as one of the pioneers in abstract art. She regarded her paintings to be *sacred*[4] and believed that they contained a *spiritual message to humanity* from higher dimensions.[5] She even called them the *Fifth Gospel*.[6] As they contain a *spiritual message to humanity* from higher dimensions, Hilma

4 HaK 555, p. 69, 17 October 1906; HaK 557, p. 17, 3 May 1909; et.al.

5 HaK 557, p. 75, 30 December 1911; et.al.

6 *"Studies of the Life of the Soul,"* HaK 421–HaK 430, pp. 311 & 1057, 3 February 1917–9 July 1918; HaK 1094, p. 59, 12 December 1943; et.al.

af Klint's non-figurative paintings are hereinafter called *symbolic works*,[7] which af Klint also expresses.[8] She presented philosophical ideas and spiritual concepts in physical forms on canvas for us to contemplate and reflect upon. These philosophical ideas and spiritual concepts are conceived as two communicating vessels in her symbolic works. She made the *Invisible Visible*.

She believed that humanity carries within itself the various developing possibilities of the atom—and hereby, one may conceive even those of the universe.[9] This we may experience in her symbolic works.

Hilma af Klint was educated as an artist at the Royal Academy of Arts in Stockholm during the period 1882–1887. She started painting her symbolic works already in 1906—well before other Western artists.[10] To her, *abstraction* was a means of expression—a vehicle for conveying knowledge—all rooted in spirituality and contact with the spirits on the *Astral* plane.[11] Her means of expression were *symbolic works* in *new* color schemes and studded with *new* images, *new* forms, *new* symbols, and letters and painted in *series*.

---

7 As Hilma af Klint did not create her symbolic works to be viewed as art, the term "painting" will be used in this article as a way to describe the medium she used in creating these sacred images.

8 Regarding *The Ten Largest* works, she writes "*The works are symbolic, a large and sacred work in 10 expressions*" or in Swedish "*Arbetena är symboliska, ett stort och heligt arbetes 10-faldiga uttryck.*" HaK 556, p. 547, 19 September 1907.

9 HaK 421–HaK 430, p. 628, 2 June 1917.

10 Hilma af Klint's symbolic works, notebooks and religious items are today owned and managed by The Hilma af Klint Foundation ("the Foundation"). All of these items have been registered by the Foundation with an individual "HaK-number." References in the text below to the symbolic works, to the notebooks and to various religious items, are thus made simply by noting their respective HaK-number.

11 Horowitz, 2024, p. 40.

Hilma af Klint's symbolic works were mainly based on three aspects:

i. ***Chartography***
   She was born into a naval family. Her ancestors published the famous *Naval Charts of the Baltic Sea* and the *Marine Navigation Tables.*[12]

ii. ***Mathematics and Natural Science***
   She developed a strong interest in mathematics and in natural science, which remained with her during her entire life.

iii. ***Philosophy and Religious History***
   She studied these topics seriously during her active life and was deeply involved in Rosicrucianism, Theosophy, as well as Christianity.

Hilma af Klint believed that paintings could embody spiritual values.[13] Her symbolic works 1906–1920 were consequently from a religious point of view primarily influenced by Rosicrucianism, Theosophy, and Christianity.

Based on her exceptionally deep knowledge in art and art history, natural science, philosophy, and religious history,[14] and based on what she created during her lifetime in form of symbolic works, we may well regard her as something of a *Renaissance Person.*

---

12 Admiral Gustaf af Klint (1771–1840)—Hilma af Klint's grandfather—made the famous "*Sveriges Sjöatlas*" and his son—Hilma af Klint's uncle—Captain Erik Gustaf af Klint (1801–1846) made the "*Nautiska och Logarithmiska Tabeller.*"

See also McNab, 2024, p. 43.

13 Bashkoff, 2024, p. 15.

14 See *The Library of Hilma af Klint* in Voss, 2022, Appendix 2, pp. 315–323.

2. *Hilma af Klint as a Mystic*

Hilma af Klint lived during a period of acute changes. As a result of industrialization in Sweden, people moved from the countryside to the towns to obtain jobs—thereby becoming cut off from their tight social networks in their homesteads in the countryside. They thus often lived in solitude. Discoveries within natural sciences from the 1850s (radio waves, X-rays, etc.) made people realize that there are aspects of the world around us, that we may not perceive with our five senses. In this environment of change and reinterpretation, various religious movements shot up like mushrooms. The church lost ground. People from all levels of society became *Seekers,* searching for something new to hold on to.

Hilma af Klint was also a *Seeker*—a rather serious and critical one. In 1879, at the age of seventeen, she participated for the first time in a séance of *Spiritism* (i.e. endeavoring to contact the souls of the dead). She subsequently became a member of the *Spiritist Literature Association.* The following year, her younger sister Hermina died at the age of ten years. Hilma af Klint aspired to convince Hermina's soul that she was dead and that she had to continue to the afterworld.

However, af Klint soon considered that Spiritism was not serious enough. She saw it as a shortcut for people to receive information in advance for which they were not yet mentally ready. She left the Spiritist movement in early 1882.[15]

Hilma af Klint had contact with the *Theosophical Society* during its introductory year in Sweden (1889). This society was the European Federation

15 The modern Anglo-Saxon Spiritist Movement was founded by the Fox sisters in 1848 in Hydesville, close to Rochester, New York, USA. Allan Kardec developed a basic theoretical foundation for this movement in Europe. It may be noted, that in a meeting in New York in 1888, Margaret Fox—one of the founding sisters—revealed to the public that the "knockings," which one heard during the Spiritist séances, were in fact caused by the sisters' bending of their toes. The Spiritist Movement was in other words a hoax.

of the Theosophical Society, which Madame Helena Blavatsky established in London in 1887. When the Swedish section of the Theosophical Society-Adyar (the headquarters in India of the Theosophical Society) was subsequently established in Sweden in 1904, Hilma af Klint joined it and remained with them until her death. She participated with seventeen Works in the Theosophical World Congress held in Stockholm in June 1913.[16]

Hilma af Klint's symbolic works are studded with various *Rosicrucian* symbols. Although the Rosicrucian tenet was important to her from 1907, it has not been established whether she was a member of any specific Rosicrucian Order—as the Rosicrucian Order is a secret and closed society. Rosicrucianism was mentioned in her notebooks for the first time in 1905: "*...be the protagonist of the Rose, be the defender of innocence....*"[17] Notebook HaK 556 contains more than fifty references to Rosicrucianism. She mentioned therein in 1907 that "*I have been sent to work for the Rosicrucian world of ideas.*"[18] She also mentions in her script *Studies of the Life of the Soul* that she is "*in the service of a Rosicrucian.*"[19]

16 Rudolf Steiner, initially the head of the German Section of the Theosophical Society-Adyar, broke with them during the year-end 1912/1913. He subsequently established in Cologne the Anthroposophical Society in 1913. Its headquarter was established in Dornach, Switzerland. The operations of the Anthroposophical Society during the period 1913–1922 may be characterized to be rather tentative and searching for a distinct form. In 1923 the General Anthroposophical Society was established and took the form, that it has today.

In 1913, Rudolf Steiner held an Anthroposophical meeting in Stockholm, in competition with the Theosophical World Congress. In addition, Katherine Tingley—head of one of the Theosophical Societies in the USA—likewise held a congress in 1913 on the island of Visingsö in the Vättern Lake in Sweden. There were in other words three main competing Theosophical and Anthroposophical congresses being held in Sweden during the summer of 1913.

17 "*...bliv rosens kämpe, bliv oskuldens försvarare....*"

HaK 555, p. 1, 7 November 1905.

18 "*Jag hade blivit sänd att arbeta för Rosencreutzarnas idévärld.*"

HaK 556, p. 431, 31 December 1907.

19 "*...jag har till sist avgivit en bekännelse att jag är i en Rosencreutzares tjänst, ...*"

HaK 421–HaK 430, p. 1646, 28 January 1918.

She consistently wore a necklace with a plain silver cross, in the middle of which was engraved a rose within a circle—i.e. a Rosicrucian cross (Figure 2). The cross symbolizes the worldly. The Rose symbolizes *mystical knowledge.*[20] The Rosicrucian cross thus represents the union of these two antitheses.

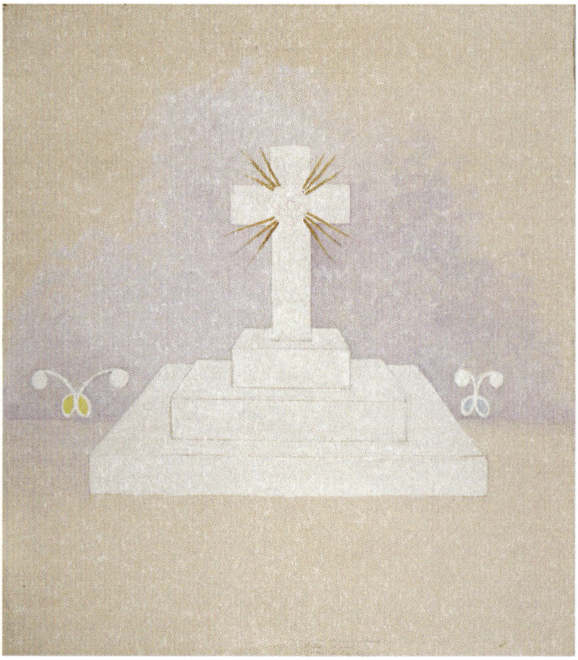

Figure 2. *The WU/Rose Series, Group III, The Large Figure Paintings, No. 9. 1907. HaK 047. Courtesy of The Hilma af Klint Foundation Photo: Moderna Museet, Stockholm, Sweden*

20 During other circumstances, Hilma af Klint means that the rose symbolizes "*the thought of the outer world*" and that the lily symbolizes "*the feeling in the outer world.*"

HaK 421–HaK 430, p. 6, 6 February 1917.

It is interesting to note, that Hilma af Klint was involved with the thoughts of Rosicrucianism well prior to learning about Rudolf Steiner's ideas of the Rosicrucians.

She joined the *Edelweiss Society* in 1896. The society was a Swedish association with an ecumenical base, established in 1890 by Huldine Beamish. As the Edelweiss Society, in the view of Hilma af Klint, did not give her the required feedback for her spiritual development, she left it already in 1897—together with four other women.[21]

These five women established the esoteric group known as *The Five* in 1896. Hilma af Klint was the youngest of these five women. The Five met regularly during the ten-year period 1896 and 1906. The Five played a *fundamental role in her spiritual development*, to make her ready in 1906 to grasp the brush and to start painting the *Drawings to the Temple*.

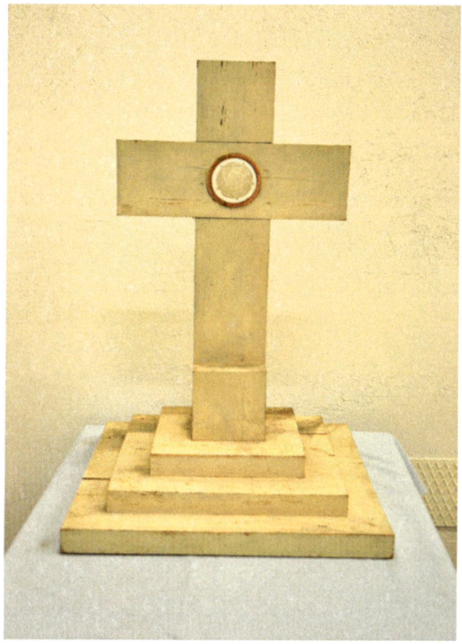

Figure 3. *The Rosicrucian Cross used by The Five during their meetings. Courtesy of The Hilma af Klint Foundation Photo: Johan af Klint*

The meetings of The Five started with a prayer, followed by meditation and a sermon in front of an altar with a triangle and a Rosicrucian cross (Figure 3). The Rosicrucian Cross stands on a base of three levels, each level representing one of the three levels that The Five must pass in their cleaning process—namely the Word, the Thought and the Mystical Knowledge (the latter

21 Matilda Nilsson, Cornelia Cederberg, Sigrid Hedman and Hilma af Klint's close friend Anna Cassel.

being symbolized by a rose wreath).[22] Thereafter, they continued with an analysis of a text from the New Testament. They also read loudly from Madame Helena Blavatsky's *The Secret Doctrine*. A spiritual séance followed, during which they contacted with spirits and spiritual leaders. The spirits had earlier informed Hilma af Klint, that she "*will receive a great gift, if she never forgets the power of the Highest.*"[23] The séances thus represented the end of their meetings.

The spiritual contacts were verbally expressed by the medium of The Five, most often by Sigrid Hedman. These contacts also gave rise to automatic writings and drawings, thirty years ahead of the Surrealists. These automatic drawings combined abstract forms with figurative elements—which later became recurring motifs in Hilma af Klint's symbolic works.[24] All these aspects are well documented in the notebooks in af Klint's estate.

Hilma af Klint arrived at the stronghold of the *Anthroposophists* in Dornach, Switzerland only in late 1920. By that time, she had already painted all her symbolic works. She studied Anthroposophy from 1922 for a few years. However, in 1930, she obtained a more nuanced view—not to mention a negative view—of the Anthroposophists. Nevertheless, she retained contacts with local Anthroposophical Societies during the balance of her life—to ascertain access to the various ideas and publications of Rudolf Steiner.

22 HaK 1156, pp. 114–115, 5 April 1898.

Martin, 2022, pp. 72–74.

The Rose wreath may in fact be a "Rosary."

23 *"Hilma får en stor gåfva, om Hilma aldrig glömmer den Högstes makt."*

HaK 1164, p. 93, the autumn of 1891.

24 In fact, the automatic drawing process probably gave Hilma af Klint the necessary incentives to unlearn the form of painting of her academic training.

Bashkoff, 2024, p. 19.

It was primarily Rudolf Steiner who was of importance to Hilma af Klint—not necessarily the Anthroposophical Society as such.

Hilma af Klint was, during her entire life, a serious *Seeker*. She was in contact with and studied the religious doctrines of the Rosicrucian Order, of the Theosophical Society, and of Christian organizations—such as the Edelweiss Association. She studied Western philosophy and esotericism, as well as, to a certain extent, Buddhism.[25] She was intrigued by Rudolf Steiner's religious thoughts when he was a Theosophist and later when he founded the Anthroposophical Society. She was thus in contact with various religious movements to the very end of her life.

Hilma af Klint's seeking brought about that she spiritually developed to a plane well above our conventional religions—in other words, close to the mental plane of the philosophers. Her library indicates that she had a strong interest during her active life in various religious movements and Western philosophy. Against this background, one may very well denominate af Klint a *Mystic*.

3. *Hilma af Klint as a Prophet*

Hilma af Klint mentions in her script *Studies of the Life of the Soul* that "*... As one of my foremost tasks is to make prophecies*"[26] and "*My mission was to explore the Astral life,...*"[27] She continues with "*I am sent to endeavor to perform a sacred task.*"[28] She also mentions that "*... I am sent to serve the Light*

25 See *The Library of Hilma af Klint* in Voss, 2022, Appendix 2, pp. 315–323.

26 "*... Ty ett av mina förnämsta uppdrag blir att profitera.*"
HaK 421–HaK 430, p. 1756, 23 February 1918.

27 "*Min mission var att utforska det Astrala livet, ...*"
HaK 421–HaK 430, p. 1079, 11 September 1917.

28 "*Jag är utsänd att försöka utföra ett heligt värv.*"
HaK 421–HaK 430, p. 2039, 29 May 1918.

and to liberate from the darkness." and "*... I am not preaching new laws, but unknown laws ...*"[29] In brief, she was given a task to perform in her lifetime, that would otherwise have taken several lives to perform.[30]

Hilma af Klint was one of the individuals, who descended from higher dimensions in order to present the knowledge to humanity about *Evolution*—i.e. the path to follow in order to be able to reach spiritual attainment—and about the concept of *Duality vs Non-Duality*. The Duality arose when God created Eve from the rib of Adam. The spirit was then broken into two halves—i.e. into two souls. One is representing Love, that was the woman, and the other Wisdom, which is the man. The soul descended into the matter to obtain experience and to process its *Karma*. This is what we express as *reincarnation*. The soul subsequently ascends to the spiritual plane, where it joins with its other half.[31] It is thus only on the physical plane, that we are divided. On the higher spiritual plane, we are ultimately *Non-Dual*. Furthermore, death may be regarded as not to exist—it only symbolizes the round trips of the soul between the spiritual and the physical worlds. These round trips lead to the expanding and a more complete life of the spirit. According to af Klint, humanity has only sixteen reincarnations left, before the two halves of the spirit finally join again and become *Non-Dual*.[32]

In addition, by letting Hilma af Klint paint the *Drawings to the Temple*, the spirits let her paint on canvas a *spiritual message to humanity* from

29 "*... jag är sänd att tjäna Ljuset och befria från mörkret.*"
"*... jag förkunnar inte nya lagar, men okända lagar, ...*"
HaK 421–HaK 430, p. 2043, 30 May 1918.

30 HaK 421–HaK 430, p. 603, 14 May 1917.

31 This has been expressed as the cyclical condition of the human soul.
Bashkoff, 2024, p. 22.

32 HaK 556, pp. 19 & 413, 5 September 1906 and 24 December 1907.
Lindén, 1999, pp. 171–182 & 266.

higher dimensions. These symbolic works should be hung and shown in a Temple, the walls of which rise higher and higher in a circular fashion. The dimensions and the vertical orientation of the symbolic works—particularly those of *The Ten Largest*—indicate that the symbolic works were designed for the interior of temples.[33] "*One of the purposes of your work is thus to obtain an independent domicile for itself, at the same time that it is brought together with as many artistic creations of others as possible.*"[34] The purpose of the Temple should thus be "*a museum to reveal the essence beyond material forces.*"[35]

Hilma af Klint mentions in 1913 that "*I will thus become a prophet, who primarily calls humanity to improve, ...*"[36] In 1941 she writes, however, that hers and Gidro's Guru informs her that "*You will never be recognized as a prophet, but your work will after your decease be subject to the wonder of humanity and it shall finally be the base for the development of many individuals.*"[37]

Against this background, Hilma af Klint may well be described as a *Prophet.*[38]

33 Horowitz, 2024, p. 41.

34 *"Ett av målen för Ditt verk är att få en självständig bostad åt verket och på samma gång låta det vara förenat med så många andras konstnärliga skapelser som möjligt."*

HaK 1084, p. 2, 8 March 1941.

35 *"ett museum för att visa vad som ligger bakom materiens krafter."*

HaK 1050, p. 6, 4 September 1932.

36 *"Jag skall således bliva en profet, som först och främst kallar mänskligheten till bättring, ..."*

HaK 572, p. 43, 21 September 1913.

37 *"Du blir aldrig erkänd som en profetissa, men Ditt verk blir efter Din bortgång föremål för människornas undran och det skall så småningom bliva till mångas utveckling."*

HaK 1083, pp. 106–107, 22 February 1941.

38 HaK 555, p. 23, 7 May 1906.

Hilma af Klint's Extraordinarily Strong Inspiration

Hilma af Klint thought that there are seven spiritual planes surrounding us.[39] The three most prominent planes for the purpose of this article are:

(i) the *Mental* plane (where there is neither any form, nor any substance).
(ii) the *Astral* plane (where there is form, but no substance).
(iii) our *Physica*l plane (where there are both form and substance).[40]

Hilma af Klint believed that the *High Masters* lived on the *Mental* plane, thus in an entirely mental environment. The High Masters could neither be seen, nor have any names. The High Masters conveyed their messages to the spirits on the *Astral* plane. These spirits could be seen, but they could not be touched. They had names such as Amaliel, Ānanda, Gregor, etc.[41] The task of the spirits was to convey the messages of the High Masters down to humanity on the *Physical* plane.

39 In fact, she adopted the thought of seven different planes from the Theosophical Society. These planes are in succeeding order the *Physical* plane, the *Etheric* plane, the *Astral* plane, the *Mental* plane, the *Buddhic* plane, the *Nirvāṇic* plane, the *Paranirvāṇic* plane and the *Mahāparanirvāṇic* plane.

Say, 2022, p. 144 and Henderson, 2023, p. 173.

40 Please note, that we have purposely refrained from mentioning here the *Etheric* plane, which is referred to in Point V on page 51.

41 HaK 1162, p. 158, 21 February 1905.

These spiritual planes are noted and presented in af Klint's various symbolic works, such as in the *Tree of Knowledge* series from 1913–1915[42] and in the *Parsifal* series of 1916.[43] Please note that she has placed the *Mental*, the *Astral*, and the *Physical* planes in the root system of the *Tree of Knowledge* (Figure 4). We will revert to this aspect in the *Intermediary Comments* below.

The idea of various spiritual planes is not unique. The Theosophists and the Kabbalah believe in seven spiritual planes. In Buddhism, it is believed that twenty-eight heavens exist—one above the other—organized in three main groups.

Hilma af Klint was promised to perform a lifework in the form of paintings based on a new method.[44] For this to be possible, she had to have an extraordinarily strong inspiration. From November 1906, she started painting in entirely *new* color schemes, with *new* symbols, with *new* forms and with *new* images and texts included in the symbolic works. How could she suddenly paint these entirely *new* works in *long series* and in *perfect form* from the outset during such *brief time periods?* The first 111 symbolic works of the *Drawings to the Temple* she painted during only one and a half years (November 1906 to April 1908)—which means around five days on average for each painting (including *The Ten Largest*). This is an incredibly prolific task for one person to execute— although she enjoyed the assistance of some friends regarding the largest symbolic works.

Dr. Marco Pasi[45] proposes, for instance, that Hilma af Klint's extreme creativity may be explained by her connection with esotericism.[46]

42 HaK 133–139, The *Tree of Knowledge* series.

43 HaK 202–350, the *Parsifal* series.

44 HaK 421–HaK 430, p. 617, 16 May 1917.

45 Dr. Marco Pasi is Associate Professor in History of Hermetic Philosophy at the University of Amsterdam, The Netherlands.

46 Pasi, 2015, pp 113–114.

Esotericism may namely offer the artist "*a controlled and institutionalized space for practicing creative dissociation,*[47] *and a convenient cultural framework for experiencing alienated agency.*"[48] Having undergone the alchemic

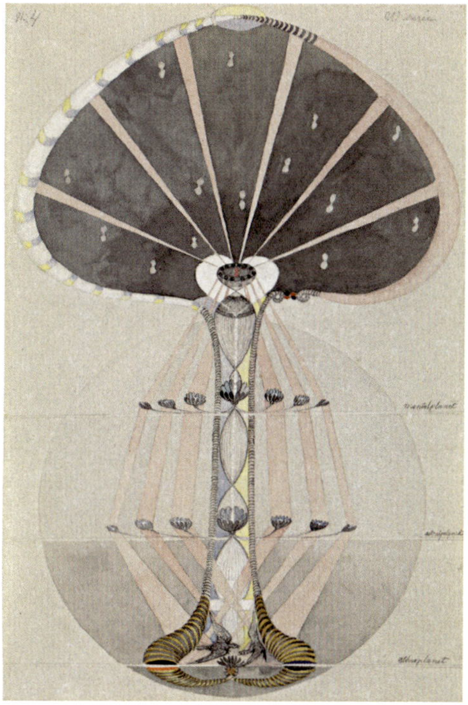

Figure 4. *The W Series, The Tree of Knowledge (Version I), No. 4.*
1915. HaK 136.
Courtesy of The Hilma af Klint Foundation
Photo: Moderna Museet, Stockholm, Sweden

47 The concept of "creative dissociation" was in fact developed by the American psychologist Michael Grosso (1997), who proposed that an experience of disintegration of the self may produce, by means of a subsequent reconstruction process, exceptional outbursts of creativity.

Pasi, 2015, p. 114.

48 The concept of "alienated agency" is according to Pasi, that the ultimate authorship of a strongly innovative or radical artistic discourse is attributed to entities subjectively independent from the author's self.

Pasi, 2015, p. 113.

cleaning process and its recreation phase, she should thus have obtained periods of exceptional creativity—as described by the *creative dissociation*. In addition, she should by means of her mediumistic approach have attributed a certain freedom in her artistic creativity to a spiritual entity other than herself—as described by the *alienated agency*.

Hilma af Klint herself meant in fact, that she was influenced as a *medium* concerning certain series. When she painted the Group III[49] she claimed that "*Over my easel I saw the sign of Jupiter, which shone strongly and appeared during several seconds. Thereafter the work started immediately. The work was executed in a manner that the pictures were painted directly through me, without any preparatory designs and with great force.*"[50]

However, the idea that af Klint acted as a *medium* in creating her symbolic works may be questioned, despite her stating several times in her notebooks that she was a medium. This skepticism may be based on various factors, such as:

- No direct orders were given to her by the spirits.
- The communication with the spirits took the form of discussions with exchanges of views. On at least one occasion, Hilma af Klint was able to have the spirits change their mind. (Figure 5)[51]
- In addition, her works were often preceded by preparatory drafts.

---

49 HaK 38–HaK 47, Group III, *The Large Figure Paintings* from 1907.

50 *"Över mitt staffli såg jag ett Jupitertecken, vilket kraftigt upplystes och visade sig under flera sekunder. Därefter begynte omedelbart arbetet, vilket skedde sålunda att bilderna målades genom mig direkt, utan föregående teckning och med stor kraft."*

HaK 556, p. 274, 14 May 1907.

51 In painting HaK 73, *The Evolution*, No 5 from 1908, Hilma af Klint managed to have the spirits change their mind and to agree that the white dog should be added to the work.

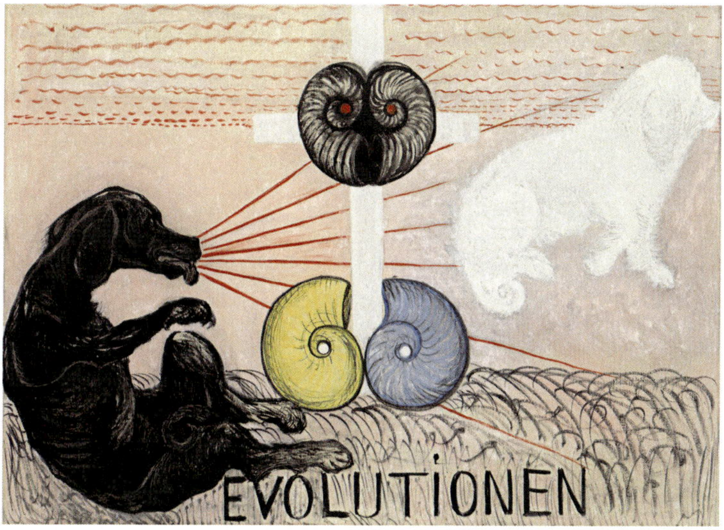

Figure 5. *The WUS/Seven-Pointed Star Series, Group VI, The Evolution, No. 5. 1908. HaK 073.*
Courtesy of The Hilma af Klint Foundation
Photo: Moderna Museet, Stockholm, Sweden

- On the completed paintings, one may also see outlines of various forms drawn with a pencil before the actual painting process.
- The spirits wanted her to work for them "*...not as a medium, but in an independent manner.*"[52]
- She also meant that "*It was not that I should blindly obey the Lords of the Mysteries, but that I should imagine them always standing next to me....*"[53]

52 "*...ej mediumistiskt, men självständigt få arbeta för vår idé,*"

HaK 557, p. 60, 27 March 1910.

53 "*Det var ej så att jag blint skulle lyda de höga Mysteriernas Herrar, utan jag skulle tänka mig att de alltid stode vid min sida,....*"

HaK 556, p. 557, 29 November 1907.

- Finally, the spirits exclaimed in 1908 that "... *you have now fulfilled such a wonderful work, that if you understood it, you would fall on your knees.*"[54]—a statement that the spirits would not have made, had they led her hands and had she thus been a proper medium to them.

Hilma af Klint's capacity to paint the *Drawings to the Temple* in such a rapid and perfect manner, without any corrections, was instead due to her extraordinarily strong contacts with the spirits on the *Astral* plane. The *colors, forms and images,* that she saw there, may be seen as messages from the High Masters. These High Masters may be nothing but a periphrasis of the *Ākāśa-Chronicle*[55] or of the Buddhist *Ālāyavijñāna*[56] in the realm of the *cosmic potentiality.*

According to af Klint, this extraordinary inspiration was based on her direct contacts with the spiritual beings on the *Astral* plane, as well as being based on her capability to mentally ascend to and descend from the *Astral* plane. The spirits claim in fact that "*We are those who inspire all artists, we give them what they believe that they themselves thought out....*

54 "... *Du har nu fullbordat ett så härligt arbete, att om Du förstod det, skulle Du falla på Dina knän.*" HaK 556, p. 542, 24 April 1908.

55 The *Ākāśa-Chronicle* (*Ākāśa* means "space" in Sanskrit) is in Indian religion and in Theosophy the denomination of a Chronicle of Time, in which is registered all events since the beginning of creation. All these events in the universe are automatically registered in an "energy matrix"—i.e. in a registry on a non-physical level of subsistence.

See also Høgsberg & Rudbøg, 2020, p. 89.

56 The Buddhist *Ālāyanavijñāna* (the Store Consciousness) is the foundation of all consciousness, and it contains impressions (*saṅkhāra*) of all our past actions. It contains the dormant pure seed of the *bodhicitta* (the Buddha-nature inherent in all sentient beings), as well as the defiled seed from discriminative cognition.

It is a wonderful interplay between the Astral world and the Physical world. By means of your work, you are in fact in the process of explaining it."[57]

She claims that her invisible spiritual teacher had informed her in 1906, that "*Eternal Sanskrit is safeguarded in the Astral world, from where the outlines are fetched to the works, that we wish to receive.*"[58] It was also mentioned that the works of certain series were supervised by the High Masters themselves—by using the *Brothers of the White Cross.*

Hilma af Klint also mentions "*... I understand that I have been sent by the Brothers and Sisters of the White Cross ... and that they without doubt stand by my side.* "[59] The *Brothers of the White Cross* is a sacred society with representatives from various religions, such as Buddha, Christ and the *Brothers of Ararat.* The *Brothers of the White Cross* are initiated in the secrets of the area of thought.[60] The spirit Gregor protects the chalice of the Truth and is a Lightbody belonging to the *Brothers of the White Cross.*[61]

The *Brothers of Ararat*—thirty in number—are "*Rosicrucians, being led by the spirit Amaliel.*"[62] The *Brothers of Ararat* have attained clear-sightedness

57 *"Vi äro de som inspirera alla konstnärer, vi giva dem vad de tro sig själva uttänka.... Det är en underbar växelverkan mellan astralvärlden och den fysiska världen. Den håller Du på att förklara genom Ditt arbete."*

HaK 1072, pp. 104–105, 1 June 1934.

58 *"Evig sanskrit bevaras i Astralvärlden och därifrån hämtas konturerna till de verk, som vi vilja ha fram."*

HaK 555, p.106, 4 February 1906.

59 *"... jag förstår att jag är utsänd från Vita Korsets bröder och systrar ... att de stå vid min sida utan tvekan."*

HaK 421–HaK 430, p. 553, 1 May 1917.

60 HaK 421–HaK 430, p. 1023, 28 August 1917.

61 HaK 421–HaK 430, p. 1500, 30 December 1917.

62 HaK 556, pp. 114, 365 & 431, 4 February 1906, 1 September 1907 and 31 December 1907.

and use the power of the Light in order to fight back the worldly life.[63] They are also initiated in the secrets of the emotional life.[64] They live in the *Astral* world.[65]

All these individuals—i.e. the *Brothers of the White Cross* and the *Brothers of Ararat*—supported af Klint in her work.

Membership in the *Brothers of Ararat* obliges in perseverance concerning the fight against arrogance and physical weakness. Membership in the *Brothers of the White Cross* obliges to bringing clarity in the reasons for both these characteristics. Georg was chosen by the *Brothers of the White Cross*. He wears a blue cloak with a white lining, a knight helmet, and armor. His helmet is decorated on top with the dove.[66] He is also said to have belonged to the Rosicrucian Order.[67]

In this manner, Hilma af Klint was informed of matters from the *Mental* plane of the spiritual world by the named spirits from the *Astral* plane—Amaliel, Ānanda, et.al.[68]

This explains Hilma af Klint's powerful inspiration. Her symbolic works were, in other words, *"copies" of what she visualized on the Astral plane—namely, the colors, the forms, the symbols, and the images of the realm of cosmic potentiality.*

63 HaK 421–HaK 430, pp. 431, 548 & 1660, 2 April, 1 May 1917 and 31 January 1918.

64 HaK 421–HaK 430, p. 1023, 28 August 1917.

65 HaK 1040, p. 8, Undated.

66 HaK 421–HaK 430, pp. 1549 & 1617, 9 January 1918 and 22 January 1918.

67 HaK 421–HaK 430, p. 1698, 12 February 1918.

68 HaK 1162, p. 158, 21 February 1905.

Hilma af Klint's Various Phases of Symbolic Works

After several years of spiritual exercise by The Five, the spirits started making recurrent references to an important mission lying ahead. In 1904, the spirit Ānanda predicted the creation of future paintings, which af Klint assumed would be from the *Astral* plane.[69] In fact, she subsequently writes that "*The work was believed to have passed from OH (Geisterland)*[70] *through the Astral world …*"[71] The spirit Georg also foresaw in January 1904 the building of a future Temple, a prediction he repeated in November that same year. He mentioned that af Klint would be requested to make the necessary architectural drawings for this Temple.[72] Later on in August 1905, she received a promise, that she should be prepared to present a message and to take part in the construction of a Temple.[73] On the same day, she was also promised, that she would work in the services of the Mysteries.[74] On a direct question, she was informed in December 1905 that her mission would be performed in the area of painting.[75]

69 HaK 418, p. 125, 18 January 1907.

70 Geisterland equals "the *Mental* plane" referred to above.

71 "*Arbetet tänktes passera från OH (Geisterland) genom Astral världen …*" HaK 556, p. 353, 21 August 1907.

72 HaK 1162, pp. 61 & 113, 12 January 1904 and 1 November 1904.

73 HaK 555, p. 2, 18 August 1905.

74 HaK 555, p. 2, 18 August 1905; and HaK 418, p. 00, 18 August 1905.

75 HaK 555, p. 4, December 1905.

On January 1, 1906, Hilma af Klint received the task to paint the *Drawings to the Temple* by the spirit Amaliel. "*Amaliel offered me a work and I answered immediately Yes. This was the large work, that I was to perform in my life.*"[76]

Hilma af Klint believed: "*The secret with the world system was to be able in an ever richer color scheme to describe God Almighty himself—thus to make him visible.*"[77] The above task from Amaliel was perhaps the method to do this.

Thereafter followed the predicted genuine purification period for three months[78]—resembling an alchemic cleaning process.[79] Restored after this purification period, Hilma af Klint was ready in November 1906 to start her painting odyssey of presenting the spiritual world to our physical world. In her own words, "*The main idea of the task was to present to humanity pictures of the life, that exists beyond everything.*"[80]

76 "*Amaliel erbjöd mig ett arbete och jag svarade ögonblickligen Ja. Det blev det stora arbetet som jag utfört i mitt liv.*"

HaK 555, p. 8, 1 January 1906.

77 "*Hela hemligheten med världssystemet är således att kunna i ett allt rikare och rikare färgspel beskriva Gud Allsmäktig själv, göra honom åskådlig.*"

HaK 421–HaK 430, p. 387, 29 March 1917.

78 HaK 1156, p. 115, 5 April 1898.

79 HaK 555, p. 2, 8 August 1905.

80 "*Uppdragets bärande idé var att delgiva mänskligheten bilder av det liv som existerar bakom allt.*" Müller-Westermann, 2020, p. 29.

Hilma af Klint performed the *Drawings to the Temple* in series and by using a symbolic language (circles, triangles, squares, spirals, etc.),[81] which was and still is enigmatic. This symbolic language is not extraordinary for af Klint. We find it also in the *maṇḍalas,* in the Tibetan temple paintings, in the rose windows of the Gothic cathedrals, in the sand paintings of the Indians, etc.[82] Her symbols have a strong archetypal tone and evoke complexes related to Anima/Animus.[83]

She also used a variety of colors, which had not previously been used by other artists. These colors included a combination of orange, lilac, pink, and dark blue (Figures 6–9). Her colors were presented in bright and soft tones. In addition to the various *forms and images*, these colors were also used as background colors for some of the paintings. As indicated above, she received information about these colors, forms, symbols, and images on the *Astral* plane. She believed that structures on higher spiritual planes also had forms. She sought in fact, to describe these symbols in her notebook HaK 1040. But as several of these symbols had a multitude of meanings depending on the circumstances, Hilma af Klint was herself unable to properly interpret the *Drawings to the Temple*.

81 The "circle" often represents the spirit, the heaven, the wholeness and the eternal.

The "white circle with a black dot in the center" symbolizes the emotional life.

The "ellipse" represents the Ether-body.

The "triangle" represents the ethereal and the pure spiritual.

The "square" represents the physical body, the earth, vitality and feelings.

The "spiral" was similar to that of the Fibonacci sequence—Nature's Code.

The "spiral" also represents evolution.

HaK 421–HaK 430, p. 408, 30 Mars 1917; Bauduin, 2018, p. 188; Burgin, 2018, pp. 246 ff; and Høgsberg R Rudbøg, 2020, p. 85.

82 Lindén, 1999, pp. 183–184.

83 Andrigo Moreira, 2020, p. 40.

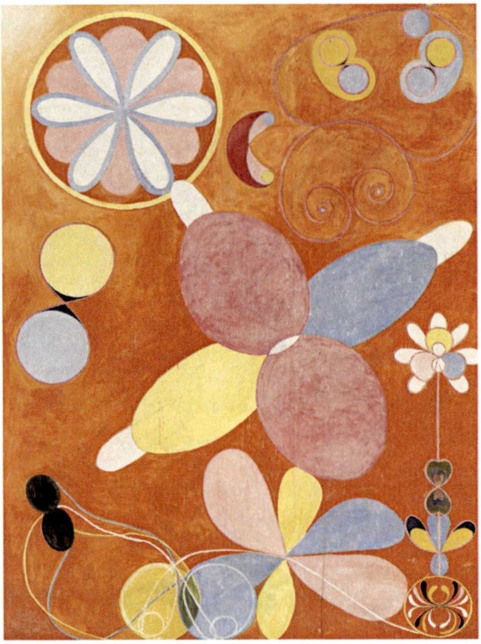

Figure 6. *Group IV, The Ten Largest, No. 4, Youth. 1907. HaK 105. Courtesy of The Hilma af Klint Foundation Photo: Moderna Museet, Stockholm, Sweden*

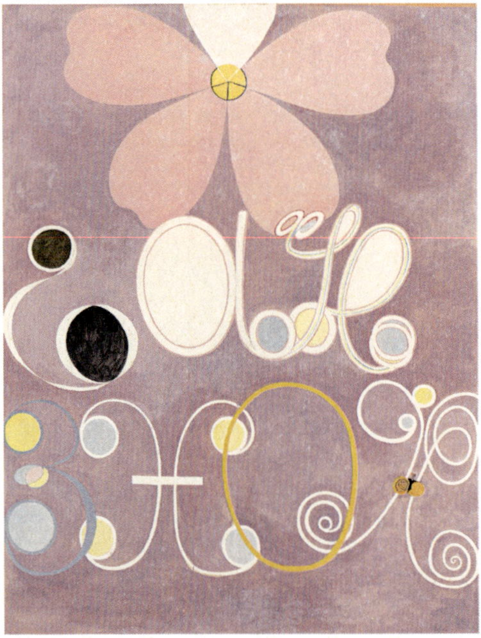

Figure 7. *Group IV, The Ten Largest, No. 5, Adulthood. 1907. HaK 106. Courtesy of The Hilma af Klint Foundation Photo: Moderna Museet, Stockholm, Sweden*

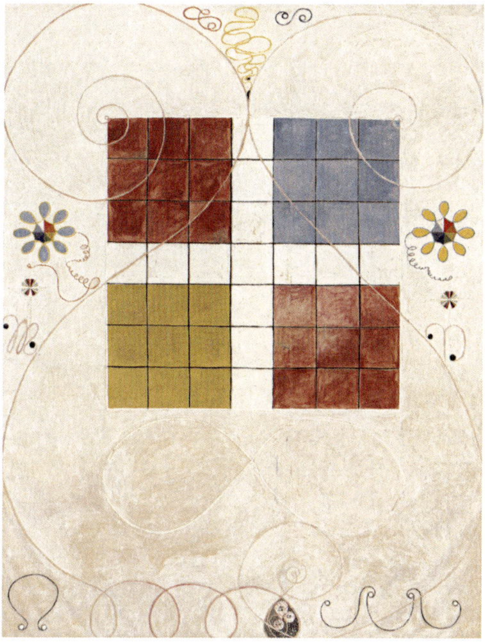

Figure 8. *Group IV, The Ten Largest, No. 10, Old Age. 1907. HaK 111. Courtesy of the Hilma af Klint Foundation Photo: Moderna Museet, Stockholm, Sweden*

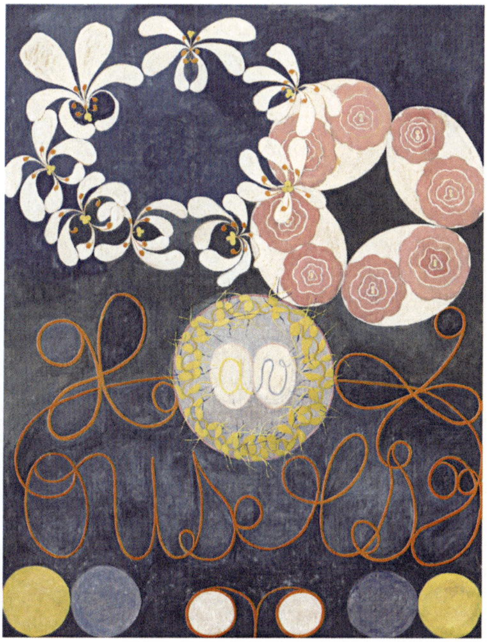

Figure 9. *Group IV, The Ten Largest, No. 1, Childhood. 1907. HaK 102. Courtesy of The Hilma af Klint Foundation Photo: Moderna Museet, Stockholm, Sweden*

As a reflection of her family background, we may experience in some of Hilma af Klint's symbolic works that their structures seem to have been influenced by *cartography* (Figure 10).[84]

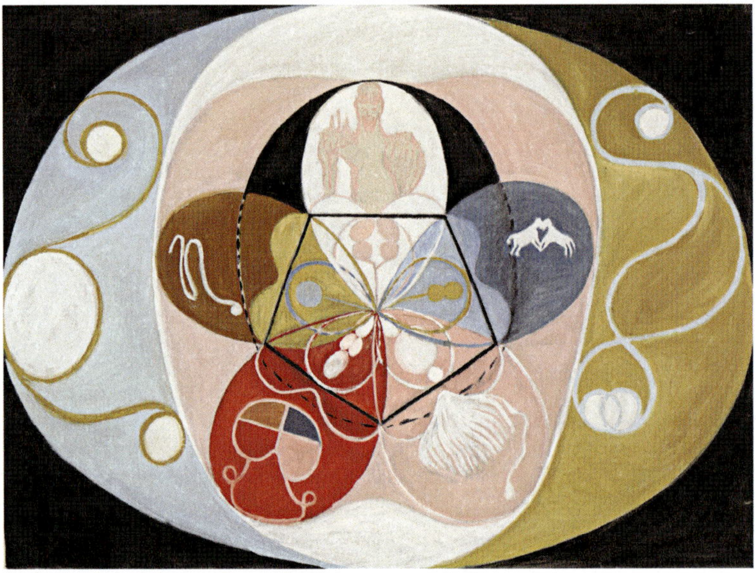

Figure 10. *The WUS/Seven-Pointed Star Series, Group VI, The Evolution, No. 14. 1908. HaK 082.*
Courtesy of The Hilma af Klint Foundation
Photo: Moderna Museet, Stockholm, Sweden

84 See for instance also the symbolic work HaK 171, The SUW Series, Group IX, *The Swan*, No. 23. 1915.

In addition, her interest in *natural science* has also affected some of her symbolic works. Hilma af Klint may even have been influenced by Thomas Young (1773–1829) and his light experiments (Figure 11).[85]

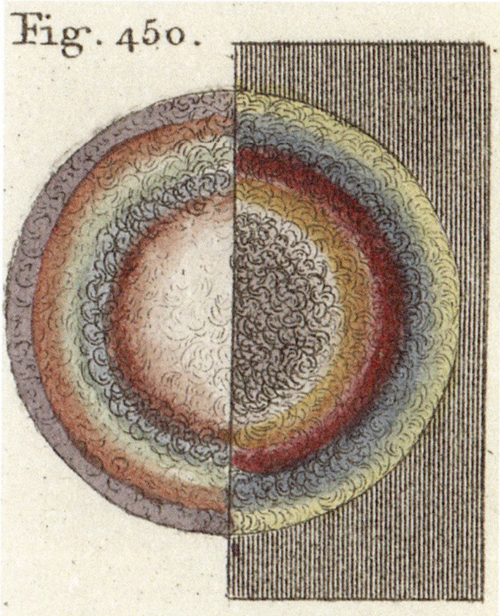

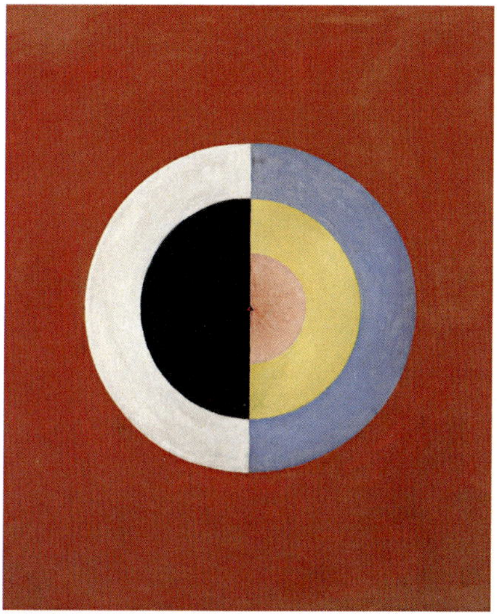

Figure 11. *Thomas Young (1773–1829). A Course of Lectures on Natural Philosophy and the Mechanical Arts, Volume 2, Plates Fig. 450 (1807). New edition with References and Notes. London: Taylor and Walton, 1845, p. 309. Courtesy of The American Institute of Physics Photo: The American Institute of Physics*

*Hilma af Klint (1862-1944)
The SUW Series, Group IX,
The Swan, No. 17. 1915. HaK 165.
Courtesy of The Hilma af Klint Foundation
Photo: Moderna Museet, Stockholm, Sweden*

85 Lundgren, 2024, fig. 4.

It is also noteworthy that Hilma af Klint used the concept of the *Fourth Dimension* (Figure 12) to show how matter and spirit meet. The Fourth Dimension is the concept where science, mathematics, and Theosophy intersect. The Fourth Dimension is presented specifically in the *US* series and in the *Swan* series.[86]

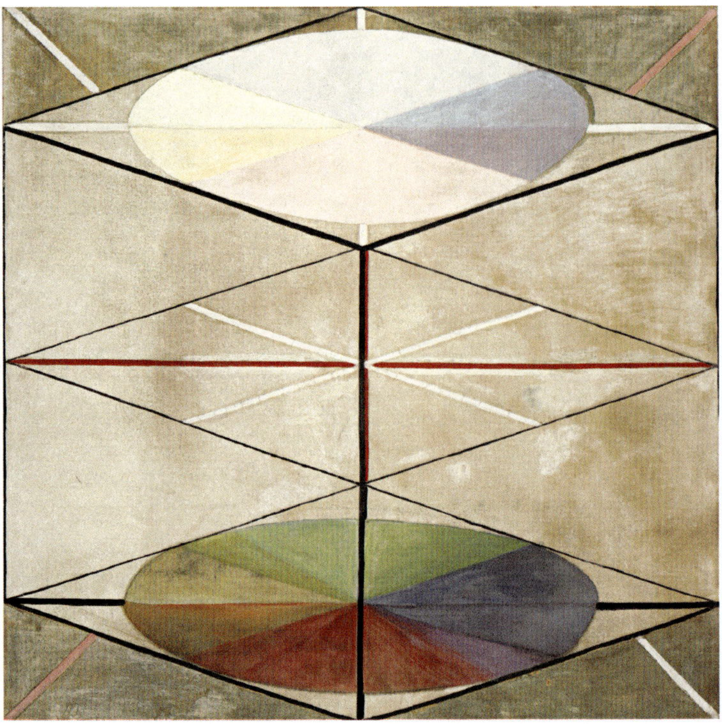

Figure 12. *The SUW Series, Group IX, The Swan, No. 23. 1915. HaK 171.*
Courtesy of The Hilma af Klint Foundation
Photo: Moderna Museet, Stockholm, Sweden

86 HaK 129–130, *The US Series* and HaK 170–171, *The Swan* series. Henderson, 2019, pp. 82–86; and Villari, 2024, p. 184.

Quantum Physics may be seen to be illustrated in *The Dove* series, where the dove, using light or vibrating strings, seems to create matter (Figure 13).[87]

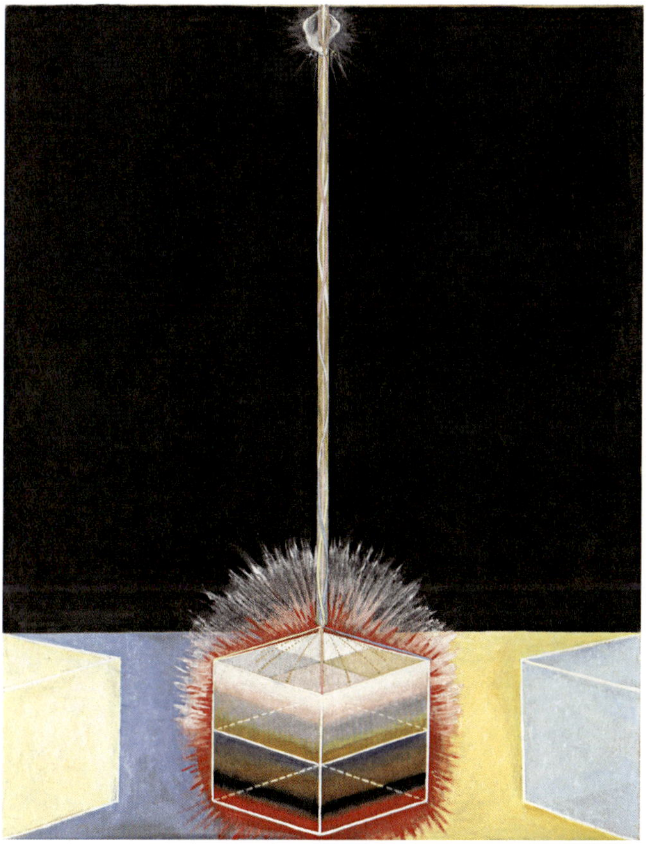

Figure 13. *The UW Series, Group IX, The Dove, No. 3. 1915. HaK 175. Courtesy of The Hilma af Klint Foundation Photo: Moderna Museet, Stockholm, Sweden*

87 Symbolic work The UW Series, Group IX, *The Dove*, No. 3. 1915. HaK 175.

In effect, according to the Quantum Physics, "*something may come into existence out of nothing,*" if only the Quantum Laws may prevail.

Rose, 2017, p. 174.

During the ensuing four-year period (1908–1912) af Klint studied *Western philosophers*, as well as Madame Helena Blavatsky's Theosophical work *The Secret Doctrine*.[88]

In 1912 Hilma af Klint resumed painting symbolic works. Between 1912–1915 she completed the *Drawings to the Temple*, which constitute 193 symbolic works all in all. The *Drawings to the Temple* is the central work, that she painted. It contains the *spiritual message to humanity* from higher dimensions. In her own words: "*My mission, if it succeeds, is of great significance to humankind. For I am able to describe the path of the soul from the beginning of the spectacle of life to its end.*"[89] The *Drawings to the Temple* expresses thus humanity's spiritual evolution and unity beyond duality and the material world. In these symbolic works, the series *Evolution* expresses the path to follow, so as to be able to reach spiritual attainment.

The *Drawings to the Temple* was painted in two stages. The first stage (1906–1908) treats the relationship *Materia-Spirit* (*WU*). The second stage (1912–1915) deals with the relationship *Spirit-Materia* (*UW*). The latter presents the Evolution seen from a cosmic and spiritual plane. These two parts are connected by means of the series the *Tree of Knowledge* (1913). The *Tree of Knowledge* could be regarded as the World Tree of the Norse Mythology—Yggdrasil—which serves as a link between the

88 See *The Library of Hilma af Klint* in Voss, 2022, Appendix 2, pp. 315–323.

89 Cited in Tate Modern, 2023, Exhibition Guide, # 10—Hilma af Klint, 2017.

seven worlds.[90] On the trunk of the *Tree of Knowledge*, in its branches, in the depth of its roots, we may observe the various phases of Evolution. In other words, we may observe how the spirit is parted into two souls; how the souls incarnate in the matter; how wisdom develops in our bodies; how the two duals are joined into Non-Duality. All this takes place under the *Holy Grail* with the infinity symbol ∞ inside on the top of the *Tree of Knowledge*. The Holy Grail continuously provides the roots with the flowing water from the original source.[91]

Hilma af Klint believed that everything has a physical body, as well as a spiritual one—both being equally natural and real. With this in mind, she analyzed during the period 1916–1920 the world around her—living matters, material matters, as well as atoms and religious movements. In 1916, she also painted the *Parsifal* series, encompassing 144 symbolic works, wherein *Parsifal* is looking for the Holy Grail on successively higher levels of consciousness.[92]

90 HaK 421–HaK 430, p. 34, 13 February 1917; see also Villari, 2024, pp. 84–85.

Please note, though, that one finds the concept of a *Tree of Knowledge* being used in other religions as well, such as:

- The *Bodhi Tree* in Buddhism (under which Buddha received the Enlightenment);
- The *Sung Ming Shu*—the Chinese Holy Tree—the Tree of Life;
- The *Arasa Maram*—*Viśnu's* tree in Hinduism;
- The two trees in Christianity; viz.
  - The *Tree of Knowledge of Good and Evil* (in the Garden of Eden); and
  - The *Tree of Life* (the Cross of Christ).

91 Lindén, 1999, pp. 168–172.

92 HaK 202–350, the *Parsifal* series from 1916.

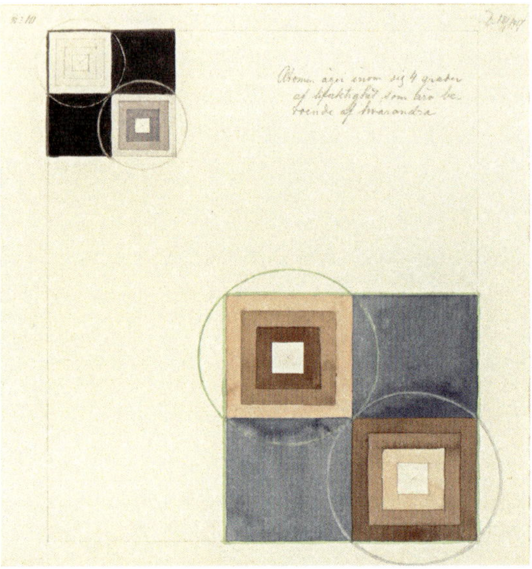

Figure 14. *The Atom Series, No. 10. 1917. HaK 362. Courtesy of The Hilma af Klint Foundation Photo: Moderna Museet, Stockholm, Sweden*

The analytical series of the *Atom* (Figure 14),[93] of the *Religions,*[94] and of *Violet flowers with guidelines* (Figure 15) may well be mentioned here. In many of these works there is a small diagram feature, indicating on which spiritual plane the analyzed object belongs.

In 1921 Hilma af Klint paused her artistic undertaking and studied Johann Wolfgang von Goethe's *Color Theory,* which Rudolf Steiner had edited.[95] In 1922 she resumed painting, this time in watercolors in the form of floating colors (i.e wet-on-wet), a technique also used in Anthroposophical art. However, af Klint developed her unique style, for instance by the use of the color black, which is proscribed in the Anthroposophical art theory (Figure 16). She pursued in this style until her last painting in 1941.

93 HaK 351–372, The *Atom Series* from 1917.

94 HaK 464–475, The series of the *Religions* from 1919/1920.

95 Prior to being elected the head of the German Section of the Theosophical Society-Adyar in 1902, Rudolf Steiner was the curator of the Goethe Foundation.

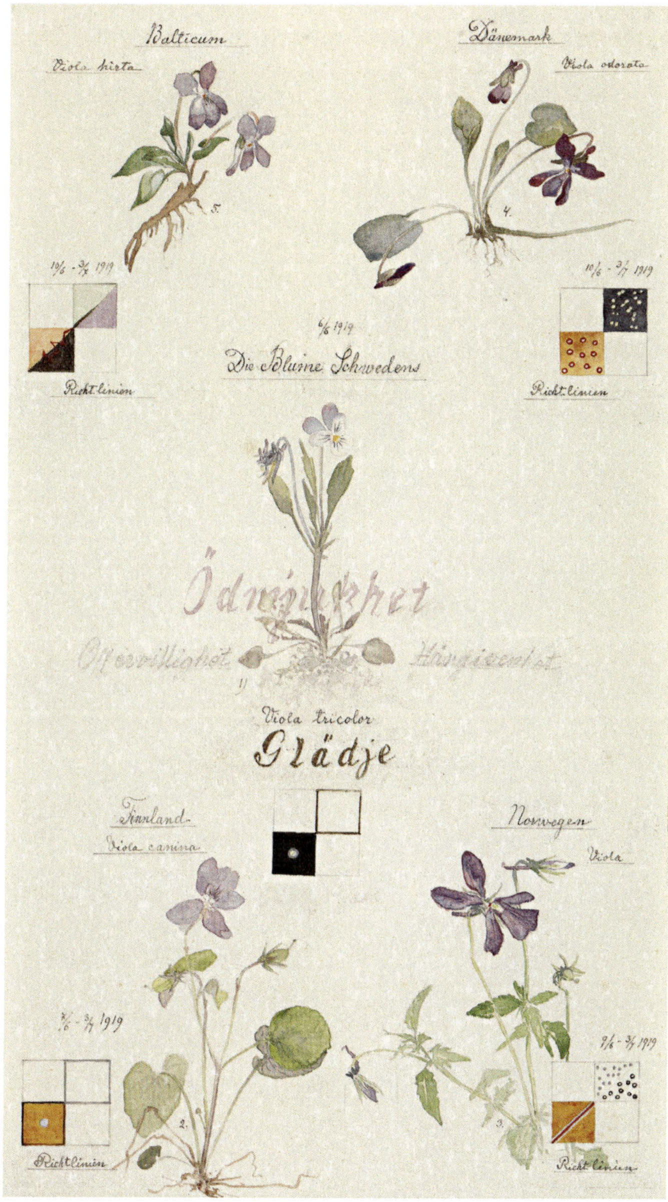

Figure 15. *The Nordic Nature Studies, Series III, Violet flowers with guidelines. 1919. HaK 457.*
Courtesy of The Hilma af Klint Foundation
Photo: Moderna Museet, Stockholm, Sweden

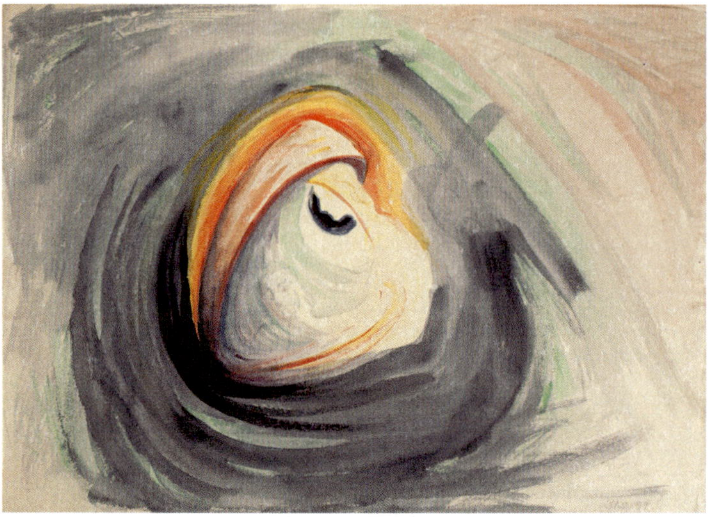

Figure 16. *Untitled, Watercolor on paper. 1932. HaK 882.*
Courtesy of The Hilma af Klint Foundation
Photo: Moderna Museet, Stockholm, Sweden

Hilma af Klint's Relationship to Rudolf Steiner

In late spring of 1908, Hilma af Klint met for the first time with Rudolf Steiner. He was then the head of the German Section of the Theosophical Society-Adyar. He was on a speech tour in Sweden and Norway. Hilma af Klint writes in her notebooks *"I had at this time no knowledge of Dr Steiner, not even that he was supposed to come to Sweden this month."*[96]

So Hilma af Klint did not know of Rudolf Steiner in March 1908. That means that she had by that time not read any of his books or written material. Nor had she learned about Rudolf Steiner's speeches about the Rosicrucian tenet, that he held at the annual congress of the Theosophical Society in Munich in May 1907. Her library contains only a few books and articles by Rudolf Steiner before 1908. She probably bought them a few years thereafter. In any event, this means that she became aware of Rudolf Steiner's ideas about the Rosicrucian tenet only at a later stage.

It is fundamental to note, that the Rosicrucian tenet meant quite a lot to Hilma af Klint. She was in contact with them *before* her contact with Rudolf Steiner and his ideas about Rosicrucian Theosophy.[97]

---

96 *"Jag hade vid denna tid ej hört talas om Dokt Steiner, ej häller att han denna månad skulle komma till Sverige."*

HaK 556, p. 522, 26 March 1908.

97 See notebook HaK 556 which has well over fifty references to the *Rosicrucians*. This notebook covers the period 4 November 1906–8 January 1908.

She subsequently met with Steiner again in 1910, at which time she might have shown him some of her symbolic works. Nothing is mentioned in her notebooks about these meetings.

Hilma af Klint held Rudolf Steiner in high esteem, as she believed that he was the individual, who perhaps could decipher *the spiritual message to humanity* embedded in her *Drawings to the Temple*. She even maintained spiritual contact with Steiner after his decease in 1925. In addition, she thought that he was the reincarnation on earth of one of the High Masters.[98]

98 HaK 1097, p. 84, 12 March 1944.

Hilma af Klint's Relationship to the Anthroposophical Society

Hilma af Klint joined the Anthroposophical Society in late 1920 and began studying its teachings in 1922. By that time, however, *all her symbolic works had already been painted.* Her research in the Anthroposophical archives at the Goetheanum center in Dornach, Switzerland had inter alia the aim of locating some material, which could be of use in deciphering the *spiritual message to humanity* inherent in her work. However, her endeavors in this respect were to no avail.

In addition, Rudolf Steiner turned down her offer in 1924 to donate the *Drawings to the Temple* to the Anthroposophical Society, to have these symbolic works adorn the rebuilt Goetheanum building.[99] Albert Steffen did likewise turn down Hilma af Klint's renewed offer after Rudolf Steiner's decease in 1925. In both cases, the reason hereto was expressed that *af Klint's symbolic works were not Anthroposophical.*

Åke Fant—the pioneer researcher of Hilma af Klint—came to the same conclusion that her *Drawings to the Temple* were "*...not a direct expression of an Anthroposophical art.*"[100]

---

99 The first Goetheanum building was burnt down at yearend 1922/1923. The present Goetheanum building was constructed 1924–1928.

100 "*... inte ett direkt uttryck för en antroposofisk konstvilja.*"

Fant, 1989, p. 230.

In 1928, af Klint participated with an unknown number of paintings in the Anthroposophical exhibition in London, *The World Conference on Spiritual Science*. She had encountered problems participating in the exhibition, as her symbolic works were deemed *"not really Anthroposophical."* At the opening of the exhibition, she gave a speech explaining the connections between her symbolic works and the Rosicrucians. However, to her chagrin, the response from the public was not up to her expectations.[101]

In 1930, af Klint had enough of the debates still ongoing in Dornach after Rudolf Steiner's death in 1925 regarding the future direction of the Anthroposophical Society. She wrote*"... then the fate of the Antr. Society is sealed."* and never returned to Dornach thereafter.[102]

During the 1930s, Hilma af Klint expressed in her notebooks rather negative views of the Anthroposophical Society, such as:

> *"At this moment dark forces rest over the Anthroposophical Society.";*[103]
>
> *"It is necessary to change the foundation of the Anthroposophical Society...";*[104] and

101 Voss, 2022, pp. 246, 250 & 331.

102 *"... därmed är Antr. Sällskapets öde beseglat."*
HaK 1047, p 33, 27 December 1930.
Voss, 2022, p. 252 and 2018, p. 60.

103 *"Antroposofiska Sällskapet har i detta ögonblick över sitt gemensamma huvud mycket mörka krafter."*
HaK 1047, p. 24, 20 December 1930.

104 *"Det är nödvändigt att omändra Antroposofins grundval..."*
HaK 1049, p. 78, 25 August 1932.

> *"The Anthroposophy has already degenerated and faith-healing forces are needed."*[105]

She even notes, that the spirits wanted *her to lead a new religious movement* that would *substitute* the Anthroposophical Society which *"is obsolete, has degenerated and is vanishing."*[106]

Despite these views, she remained a member of various local Anthroposophical Societies for the balance of her life. Hereby, she ensured access to Rudolf Steiner's ideas and written material. It is important to note, that it was Rudolf Steiner that was of importance to Hilma af Klint—not the Anthroposophical Society per se.

It should also be noted that although af Klint continued after 1930 to be a member of various local Anthroposophical Societies, she also continued for the remainder of her life to be in touch with, and member of, other religious associations, such as the Rosicrucians and the Theosophical Society-Adyar. As a mystic, she wished to exchange views with representatives of different religious faiths. A proof of this is, that the Theosophical Society-Adyar in Malmö sent a flower wreath to the funeral ceremony of Hilma af Klint in 1944—as did the Anthroposophical Society.

◆ ◆ ◆

The Anthroposophical tenet advocates that the individual using his own active development has the possibility *"to get to know the human body and*

105 *"Antroposofin har redan urartat och där behöves helbregdagörande krafter."* HaK 1070, p. 14, 7 February 1934.

106 *"... i samband med det, som är föråldrat, som urartat, sjunker undan."* HaK 1070, pp. 84–85, 17 February 1934.

its relation to heavenly wisdom."[107] The Anthroposophists strive to live in and to use the body.[108] The Anthroposophical tenet is thus based on the concept of *individual—the divine human body.*

The Theosophical tenet, on the other hand, is based on older European philosophy, like Neoplatonism. According to the Theosophical Society-Adyar, everything is based on the *divine being,* inherent in each living being. The Theosophical Society-Adyar is based on the teaching of *Karma* and on the aspect of reincarnation. The Theosophical Society-Adyar wants to *loosen man from his body* and to liberate him from it. The Theosophical tenet is thus based on the concept *the individual-spirituality (the divine wisdom).*

Hilma af Klint's Philosophy of Life lies on a plane well above our conventional religions, in other words, close to the mental plane of the philosophers. But in case her Philosophy of Life must be classified, Hilma af Klint's Philosophy of Life would be seen to be much closer to the tenets of the Rosicrucian and of the Theosophy, than it would be to that of the Anthroposophy.

◆ ◆ ◆

In conclusion, one may not regard Hilma af Klint as an active and believing Anthroposophist in the true sense of the word. She was a spiritual seeker in "mankind's wisdom" (*anthrop* and *sophia*) in a broader and deeper sense.

In addition, all of Hilma af Klint's symbolic works were already painted—long before she joined the Anthroposophical Society in Dornach in 1920.

107 *"... att komma till insikt om människokroppen och om dess ställning till himmelsk vishet."* HaK 1092, p. 64, 13 May 1943.

108 HaK 1098, p. 115, 28 July 1944.

Hilma af Klint's Philosophy of Life and Its Reflections in her Symbolic Works

Hilma af Klint was convinced that her symbolic works were pioneering and comprised an important *spiritual message to humanity* from higher dimensions—particularly the *Drawings to the Temple*. That was the reason, she kept them isolated from her conventional paintings—at the request of the spirits who stated "*Note that as long as it will be necessary, the pictures should be hidden from the eyes of the public, until the time is right to show them.*"[109] In addition, she also meant that her symbolic works, particularly the *Drawings to the Temple*, should be kept together. They were namely painted in series—which means that the entire series should be viewed, not individual symbolic works. This means that to ensure a proper interpretation of their inherent *spiritual message to humanity*, the symbolic works should be kept together. This requirement is duly reflected in the statutes of The Hilma af Klint Foundation. In conclusion, the symbolic works should thus neither be *sold*, nor be *separated*, nor be *dispersed*.

However, Hilma af Klint was herself unable to decipher the *spiritual message to humanity* inherent in the symbolic works—despite all her efforts and research in Sweden and in Dornach, Switzerland. This failure

---

109 "*Märken väl, så länge som det är nödvändigt måste bilderna gömmas undan allmänhetens ögon innan deras tid att framträda blir möjlig.*"

HaK 556, pp. 230 & 520, 2 March 1907 and 24 March 1908; and HaK 1088, p. 149, 15 March 1942.

weighed heavily upon her during her last years in life. In addition, none of the experts whom she contacted—not even Dr. Rudolf Steiner—was able to interpret her symbolic works. Indeed, nobody has to this very day been able to properly do so. The spiritual message inherent in Hilma af Klint's symbolic works will thus be a major task for future academic researchers to analyze and interpret.

These symbolic works are namely a *spiritual synthesis* in the form of paintings—similar to how we view Icons. They convey a *spiritual message*. We should thus regard them as beautiful paintings only on a secondhand basis. They should under no circumstances be commercialized. They ought to be shown continuously in a Temple for the benefit of spiritually searching individuals. Hilma af Klint suggested that the Temple should be erected on the island of Ven, outside of Landskrona in the strait of Öresund, Sweden.

By integrating insights from scientific research into her artistic practice, Hilma af Klint created a unique visual language that merges science and spirituality, offering ideas about the deeper mysteries of existence.[110]

◆ ◆ ◆

Hilma af Klint's Philosophy of Life may briefly be ascribed as:

Hilma af Klint was convinced that her symbolic works reveal another reality, beyond the visible one. Her symbolic works convey impressions from other dimensions. Her Philosophy of Life—as expressed in her symbolic works—may be conceived to be visualized in fourteen aspects: viz.

110 Villari, 2024, p. 234.

I.

Hilma af Klint believed that everything—i.e. all living beings, as well as all matter—emanates from the keynote, that sounds with its vibrations through the entire universe. Once strung, it may never cease to vibrate.

Anāhata is the heart *chakra* in the Hindu Yogic and Buddhist Tantric traditions. It contains the double triangle, that we also find in the central picture of the third *Altarpieces, No. 3*[111] (see Figure 25). In Sanskrit, *anāhata* means unhurt, unstruck, and unbeaten. *Anāhata Nad* refers to the Vedic concept of "*unstruck sound*"—i.e. the above referred to keynote of the universe or the sound of the celestial realm.[112]

Hilma af Klint mentions in her script *Studies of the Life of the Soul,* that the Primordial force within the universe is constantly in the process of developing "*new forms, new bodies and new Etheric bodies, in which Life may be introduced.*"[113]

Hilma af Klint was in other words of the opinion, that *all life and matter emanate from the keynote of the universe.*[114]

In Buddhism, one believes that this emanation—of the living beings and of the matter—is based on the *Limitless light* or on the *vibrating strings*—which is another way of describing the keynote of the universe. Natural scientists believe in the *vibrating strings,* which is the base of the so-called

111 Symbolic work HaK 189. Please also refer to the Jewish Star of David.

112 Based on the recommendation of Rachel Villari, the consideration of *Anāhata* has been added to this research and will be further developed in the future. Our discussion was held on the 20th of August, 2024.

113 *"Ständigt sysselsätter sig Urkraften med att utveckla inom universum .... nya formbildningar, nya kroppar och nya eterkroppar, i vilka Livet må kunna införas."*

HaK 421–HaK 430, p. 1803, 9 March 1918.

114 HaK 174, pp. 130 & 132, 12 May 1914.

String Theory. Emanuel Swedenborg wrote in 1719 in his book *On Vibrations,* about a cosmos, in which everything was vibrating.[115]

II.

Hilma af Klint was also affected by *Hermetism.*[116] The very first symbolic work in the initial series—the *Primordial Chaos*—of the *Drawings to the Temple*—presents that chaos and darkness constitute the source of life. In af Klint's own words, she states "*The meaning is to present a core from which the Evolution emanates under rain and storm, lightnings and storm.*" (Figure 17)[117]

III.

In Chinese *Huayan* Buddhism, all consciousness is in direct *connection* with each other and all parts are closely related and *influence* each other. af Klint writes in the upper right-hand corner of the *Atom No. 2* in the *Atom* series that "*Each atom has its central point—but that each central point is in direct connection with the central point of the universe*" (Figure 18).[118]

115 Birnbaum & Voss, 2024, pp. 74–75, 15 March 2024.

116 Hermetism is a religious-philosophical tenet with roots back to the Hermetic Corpus, a collection of texts attributed to Hermes Trismegistus, blending Greek, Egyptian and early Christian ideas. This *prisci theologi* was proposed by a line of men Hermes Trismegistus, Zoroaster, Orpheus, Aglaophemus, Pythagoras, and Plato. It became influential during the Renaissance, through translations and interpretations by thinkers like Marcilio Ficino. The *Asclepius* was known to the church fathers. The balance of the *Corpus Hermeticum* was translated by Marcilio Ficino during the 1460s. According to Hermetism, the entire universe is based on a divine singularity, from which reality emanates—i.e. the spirited universe. By various meditative practices, man may awaken the divine core in himself and by means hereof manage to avoid the reincarnation process. Heiser, 2011, pp. 9, 35–37, 43–50, 229.

117 *"Meningen är att framställa en kärna från vilken Evolutionen utgår under rägn och storm, blixt och oväder."*

HaK 556, p. 119, 7 November 1906.

118 Symbolic work HaK 354 from 1917.

"Hvarje atom har sin medelpunkt—men hvarje medelpunkt står i direkt förbindelse med universums medelpunkt."

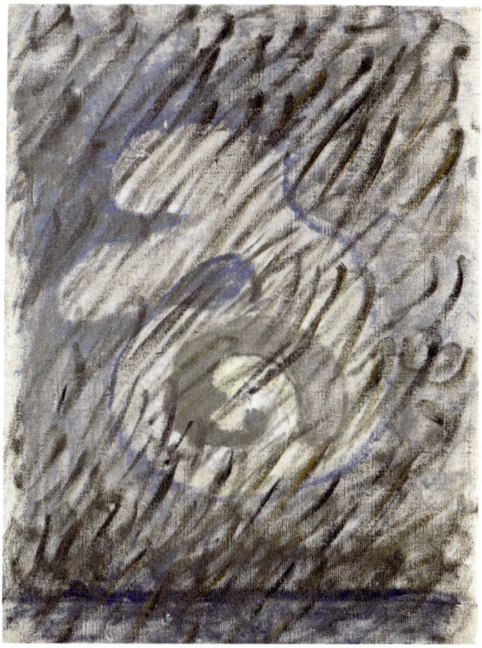

Figure 17. *The WU/Rose Series, Group I, Primordial Chaos, No. 1. 1906. HaK 001. Courtesy of The Hilma af Klint Foundation Photo: Moderna Museet, Stockholm, Sweden*

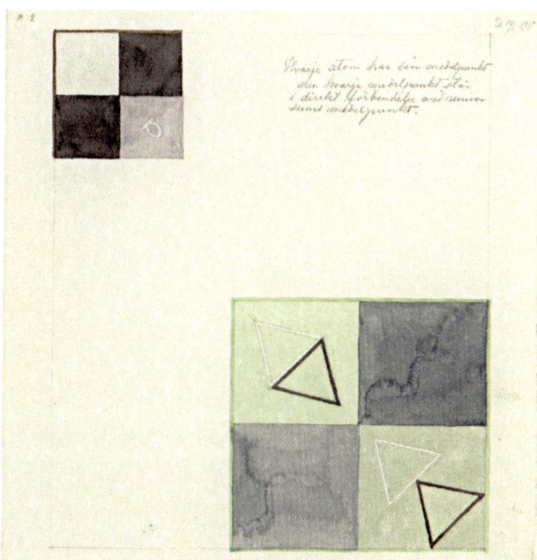

Figure 18. *The Atom Series, No. 2. 1917. HaK 354. Courtesy of The Hilma af Klint Foundation Photo: Moderna Museet, Stockholm, Sweden*

IV.

As indicated above, Hilma af Klint believed that *everything has a physical body, as well as a spiritual body—both being equally natural and real.*[119] This idea reminds us of the conversations by Plato (428–348 BCE) with Socrates—about the *world of ideas* and the *world of senses.*

According to Plato, the world of ideas is the true reality. The world of senses, on the other hand, is only a shadow of, or a bleak copy of, the world of ideas (Please refer to the *Allegory of the Cave*).[120] Incidentally, you may recall that humanity with its five senses may only experience 5% of the universe.

According to Plato, *true knowledge* may only be arrived at using *common sense*, the object of knowledge which are the *ideas*. On the other hand, the *impressions* are *fraudulent.*

This view of the two bodies is based on the Theosophical tenet. In addition, hereto, it is entirely in conformity with the *tathāgatagarbha* concept in Buddhism, particularly in the Chinese *Dàchéng qī xìn lù* (大乘起信論)—*The Awakening of Faith in the Mahāyāna.*[121]

119 HaK 1158, p. 6, 20 October 1903; & HaK 1162, p. 9, 20 October 1903.
Rose, 2017, p. 298.

120 Rose, 2017, p. 296.

121 Taishō 1666.
Taishō represents the New Edition of the Buddhist Canon compiled during the Taishō Era (30 July 1912 to 25 December 1926).

V.

Hilma af Klint believed that there was an *Etheric* plane between the *Physical* plane and the *Astral* plane. Likewise, our physical body on the *Physical* plane, was supposed to be reflected on the *Etheric* plane by an *Etheric* body—i.e. a body cleaner and more sensitive to spiritual aspects.[122]

Hilma af Klint's notebooks contain more than 2,800 references to *Ether*, with the mainstay of these references being noted in the notebooks from 1931–1944.[123]

In 1916, af Klint painted a series of symbolic works called *Parsifal*. This series consists of 144 symbolic works, organized into four groups. Group 2 encompasses four wrappers—i.e. one wrapper for each of the *Physical* plane, the *Etheric* plane, the *Astral* forces and the *Mental* plane. The *Etheric* plane consists of six symbolic works,[124] which are decorated in the center by double clams. These symbolic works are enclosed in a cover—the front cover is decorated with a gold cross, while the back cover is decorated with a silver cross.

The first symbolic work[125] of the *Etheric* plane wrapper consists of a red square decorated in the middle by dark double clams in the form of a standing trisect figure, surrounded by twelve double clams in a circle (Figure 19).

122 HaK 559, pp. 28 & 33, 13 and 17 June 1912; and p. 138, 15 August 1912.

123 The *Ether* was earlier thought to be an invisible and a transient substance that filled the entire universe. Already Aristoteles meant that the *Ether* was the fifth element after fire, earth, air and water. The *Ether* was regarded as a medium, in which light travelled. However, Einstein's Special Theory of Relativity cleared away the concept of *Ether* in 1905.

124 HaK 269—HaK 274.

125 HaK 269.

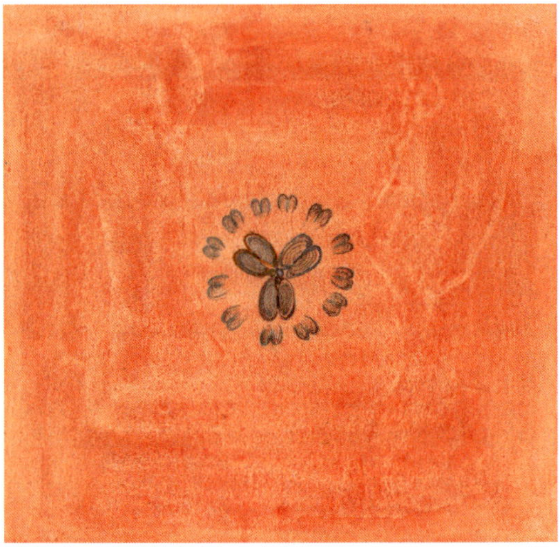

Figure 19. *The Parsifal series, Group II, The Ether Convolute, No. 60. 1916. HaK 269.
Courtesy of The Hilma af Klint Foundation
Photo: Moderna Museet, Stockholm, Sweden*

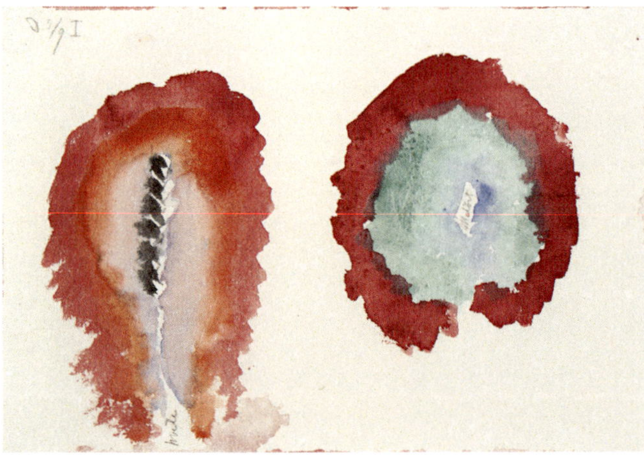

Figure 20. *On the Viewing of Flowers and Trees, Wheat and Wormwood. 1922. HaK 627.
Courtesy of The Hilma af Klint Foundation
Photo: Moderna Museet, Stockholm, Sweden*

VI.

By reading Carl du Prel, Hilma af Klint believed that contacts with the spiritual planes above were made easier using the assistance of a *transcendental subject.*[126]

VII.

Hilma af Klint was also convinced, that *all sentient beings have a soul.*[127] From 1922, she started to paint plants with an aura (Figure 20).

VIII.

Some philosophers believed that there is a *unity between matter and spirit.*[128] This view was inter alia expressed by Carl du Prel.[129] Of interest to note is that also Carl Gustav Jung had a corresponding view. He expresses this as follows:

> *It is not only possible, but fairly probable even, that psyche and matter are two different aspects of one and the same thing.*[130]

---

126 du Prel, 1890, I p. 12 and II p. 140.

127 HaK 1041, p. 56, 29 August 1941; Villari, 2024, p. 7 and Say, 2022, p. 147.

This is close to Hermetism, where the individual by means if meditative practices may arise the divine core within himself. It is also close to the *tathāgatagarbha* concept in Buddhism. Please note, that the esoteric doctrines and the Theosophists go even further and mean that ***everything*** (i.e. sentient beings ***and*** matter) has a soul.

Say, 2022, p. 145.

128 du Prel, 2023, *The Philosophy of Mysticism*, II, pp. 128–129 & 140–142.

129 This is fundamentally different from the view of René Descartes (1596–1650), who proposed ***Dualism*** with its complete distinction between soul and body.

Eidem, 2024, pp. 47–48.

130 Jung, 1960, p. 418.

However, Hilma af Klint goes one step further. She claimed that the meaning of life was to reach a unity between the two souls, to re-create the original spirit and thus to re-establish *Non-Duality* (please see the section "Prophet" on pages 13–15). One way to realize this goal was to leave the darkness of matter and change it for the refulgence of the *Etheric* body.[131]

IX.

Hilma af Klint advocated that *everything is Non-Dual* (i.e. *All is One*), which means that *Macrocosmos* and *Microcosmos* may be regarded as *Non-Dual,* as explained in the Hermetic theme "*As above, so below.*"[132] This concept is expressed in her symbolic works using complementary dual symbols such as woman/man; blue/yellow; hook/eye; etc. in order to show unity—*Non-Duality.* Symbiosis was the key to knowledge[133] and to the process of evolution.

The concept of *Non-Duality* is in fact one of the most fundamental thoughts within Buddhism—e.g. in the Chinese *Huayan* (華嚴) tradition, it is expressed that "*All is One.*" Even the extreme example *saṁsāra-nirvāṇa* may be regarded as *Non-Dual.*[134]

Baruch Spinoza (1682–1677) also proclaimed *Non-Duality* in the form that soul and body were the same. He also stated that the world was *One*, and could not be split.[135]

131 HaK 421–HaK 430, p. 1317, 14 November 1917.

132 "*Allt är Ett,*" see for instance the meaning of the "double triangle" in Picture 25.
HaK 555, p. 19, 5 September 1906.

133 Voss, 2024, p. 56.

134 It may be emphasized, that Hilma af Klint was ***not*** a Buddhist. The Buddhist concepts that pervade in her paintings, are concepts that she came across studying the Theosophical literature. The Theosophical tenet means inter alia that the entire universe (from the single atom to the galaxies) constitutes one single unit, in which every sub-unit is mutually conditioned to each other.

135 Eidem, 2024, pp. 39 & 48.

In addition, Hilma af Klint believed that it was the tension between spirit and matter; between masculine and feminine, etc. that leads to expansion and to *Unity (Non-Duality)*.

X.

Hilma af Klint believed in *Evolution*—i.e. that we by consequent acting may ultimately reach a spiritual plane.[136] But first, we need an *Involution* to have taken place (Figure 21).[137]

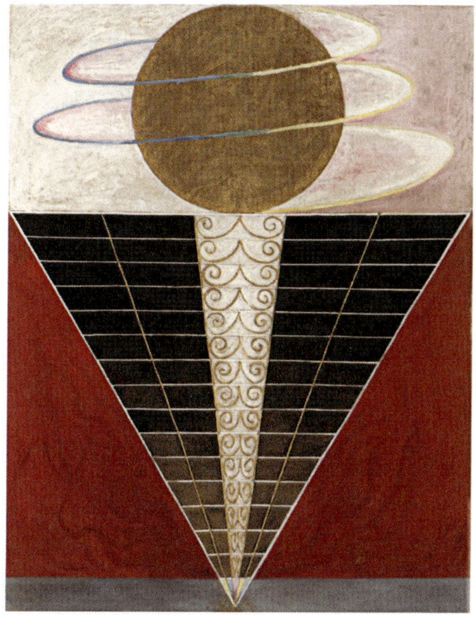

Figure 21. *Group X, Altarpieces, No. 2. 1915. HaK 188. Courtesy of The Hilma af Klint Foundation Photo: Moderna Museet, Stockholm, Sweden*

The key phrase of The Five was *Sic transit gloria mundi (Thus passes away the Glory of the World)*.[138] This keyword means that one should separate the *soul from the body*—and *the spirit from the soul*. The Self is not separated by careful cultivation of soul and body, but by the elevation of body and soul to *Ātman*. Herewith sensitive fluids are expelled, and the body and soul are hardened against the temptations of the world of the senses.[139]

136 See the *Altarpieces* series (HaK 187 & HaK 188).

137 Involution is the descent of a higher "impulse" to the lower physical form.

138 *"Pater Sancte, sic transit gloria mundi"* is a phrase, that up to 1963 was used as a *memento mori* by the newly elected Pope when he entered for the first time into St. Peter's Basilica in the Vatican.

139 HaK 556, p. 481, 22 February 1908. See also the Theosophical tenet on page 44 above.

Please note, that Buddhists do not believe in an *Ātman*—in fact in Buddhism it is believed that a *Self* does *not* exist—*Anātman*.

XI.

Hilma af Klint believed in *reincarnation*.[140] She noted in fact in her notebooks that humanity has only sixteen reincarnations left, before the two souls unite permanently into One spirit—*Non-Duality*. She indicates that this is presented by the sixteen planes in her paintings of the *Altarpieces* series (Figures 21 & 22) and by the sixteen-step ladder in painting No. 7 in the *Tree of Knowledge* series (Figure 23).[141]

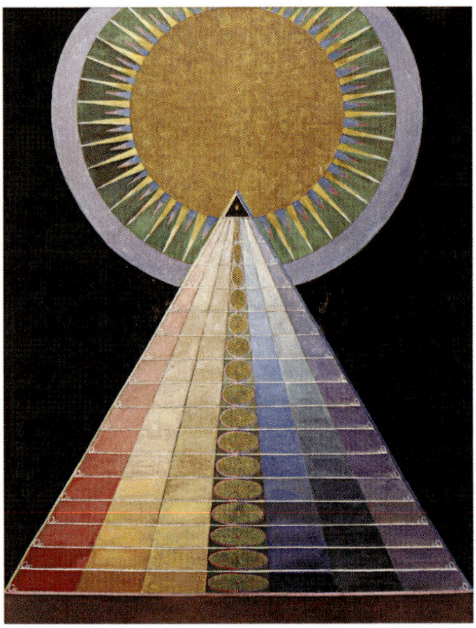

Figure 22. *Group X, Altarpieces, No. 1. 1915. HaK 187.*
Courtesy of The Hilma af Klint Foundation
Photo: Moderna Museet, Stockholm, Sweden

140 Hilma af Klint's letter to Tyra Kleen of 3 September 1943.
See also the *Altarpieces* series in Figures 21 & 22 (HaK 188 & HaK 187).

141 HaK 556, p. 133, 20 November 1906.

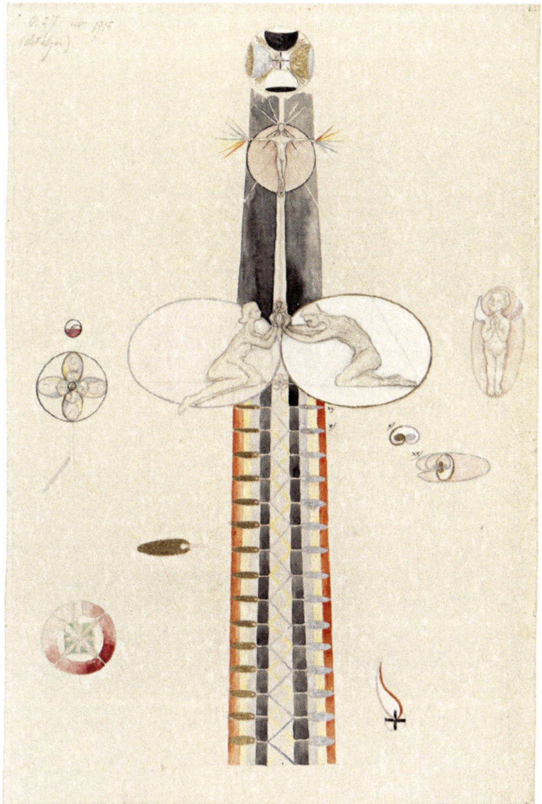

Figure 23. *The W Series, The Tree of Knowledge (Version I), No. 7b. 1915. HaK 139b. Courtesy of The Hilma af Klint Foundation Photo: Moderna Museet, Stockholm, Sweden*

XII.

In order to be released from her earthly limitations, the human being *must relinquish her emotional life in its earthly form.*[142] To paint the *Drawings to the Temple,* Hilma af Klint was herself consequently forced to completely withdraw from the world during eight years.[143]

142 HaK 421–HaK 430, p. 1239, 24 October 1917.

143 HaK 421–HaK 430, p. 1160, 5 October 1917.

XIII.

Like the Theosophists, Hilma af Klint believed that everything in the universe moves by means of a *cyclic development in spiral forms towards higher forms of existence*. To illustrate this, af Klint uses the Fibonacci spiral in her symbolic works (Figure 24).[144] The various shells in her symbolic works are examples hereof. Evolution was thus a spiritual process in spiral form guiding the soul towards divine development.[145]

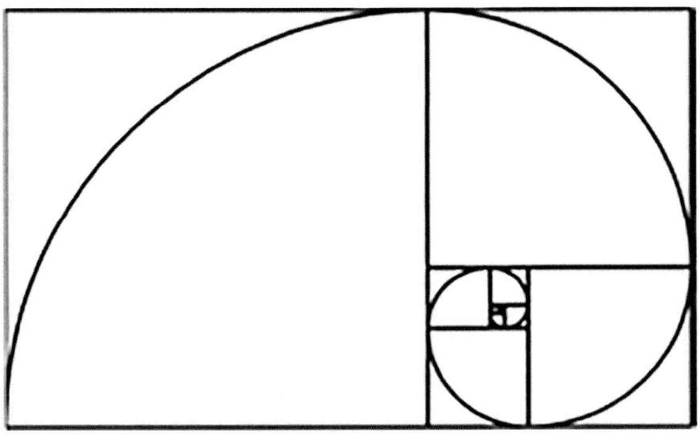

Figure 24. *The Fibonacci Spiral*
Courtesy of the Upptech AB, Jönköping, Sweden
Photo: Johan af Klint

XIV.

When *Non-Duality* has been reached, *one returns to the state of potentiality*—only soon to start a new round (*saṁsāra*), but this time presumably from a higher plane.[146]

◆ ◆ ◆

144 The Fibonacci spiral may be observed in various aspects of nature—from the simple shells and plants, to the forms of the galaxies.

145 Villari, 2024, p. 86.

146 Høgsberg & Rudbøg, 2020, p. 81.

In *Altarpieces, No. 3,*[147] the central figure (Figure 25) presents the ultimate message of Hilma af Klint's symbolic works:

- The *circle* represents totality and eternity.
- The *triangle* represents the ethereal and the purely spiritual.
- The *double triangle* symbolizes the unity of the extremes. They permeate each other and become One. *All is One.* The *double triangle* may also be seen as the hermaphrodite or the androgynous—the aim of individual perfection.

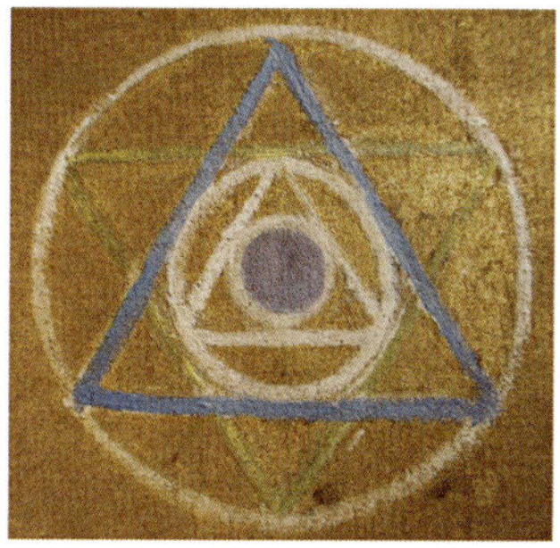

Figure 25. *Groups X, Altarpieces, No. 3 (detail). 1915. HaK 189. Courtesy of The Hilma af Klint Foundation Photo: Moderna Museet, Stockholm, Sweden*

- The indication in the figure of *further triangles* may mean, that the figure refers to the circle of transmigration (death-rebirth)—i.e. the *saṁsāra* concept.
- The *central point* may indicate *nirvāṇa.*

The figure may thus in conclusion represent the perfect Non-Dual concept—the eternal saṁsāra-nirvāṇa concept.

◆ ◆ ◆

So, one may well conclude, that while her ancestors were charting the sea, *Hilma af Klint was charting the spiritual world—making the Invisible Visible.*

147 Group X, *Altarpieces,* No. 3. 1915. HaK 189.

Intermediary Comments

Before continuing, it should be mentioned, that several different views exist concerning on what basis Hilma af Klint's symbolic works should be interpreted.

Some mean that a pure *Christian interpretation* ought to be conducted. This is inter alia illustrated on the following address:

www.hilmaafklintshemlighet.se

Given her interest in nature and in natural science—other individuals mean that *natural science* should be the basis, on which to interpret Hilma af Klint's symbolic works.

The *Kabbalah* (Figure 26) and the *Gnostic Kabbalah* have also been mentioned as suitable bases for an interpretation of Hilma af Klint's symbolic works. Please note regarding the Gnostic Kabbalah (Figure 27), that

(i) by referring to the ten Sephiroths, the seven spiritual planes are presented.
(ii) the *Mental* plane (Nezach), the *Astral* plane (Hod) and the *Physical* plane (Jesod) are all indicated at the bottom end of the *Gnostic Kabbalah*—in conformity with what Hilma af Klint indicated in the root area of the *Tree of Knowledge* (Figure 4).
(iii) above the Kether (the Crown) there exists three further Sephiroths; namely,
 * *Ain*—Nothingness,
 * *Ain Soph*—Limitless. and

* *Ain Soph Aur*—Limitless Light.
They are three aspects of the Absolute, which in synthesis may be regarded as the Unknown—of which "*no image should be made*" according to Moses. It is from this light that creation is made[148]—or as indicated by Hilma af Klint, from the *key-note of the universe.*

(iv) The *Ain Soph Aur* is Christ,[149] who must divide itself in three parts in order to manifest anything. That is the *Holy Trinity—Kether, Chochmah* and *Binah,* which are divine energy—not persons.

References could also be made to the *Limitless Light,* that in Buddhism is the fundamental source for our existence. This Limitless Light may also be ascribed as the *vibrating strings,* which constitute the foundation of the String Theory.

The above aspects are mentioned only for information purposes—without getting into further details. It is up to academic researchers to address these matters in the future.

148 Glorian, 2024, p. 5.

149 Plotinus (c:a 204–270 AD), the third century Hellenistic philosopher from Roman Egypt, believed that God was Light.

Plotinus, *The Enneads,* transl. Stephen MacKenna (Burdett, Larsson Publications, 1992)

Say, 2022, p. 72.

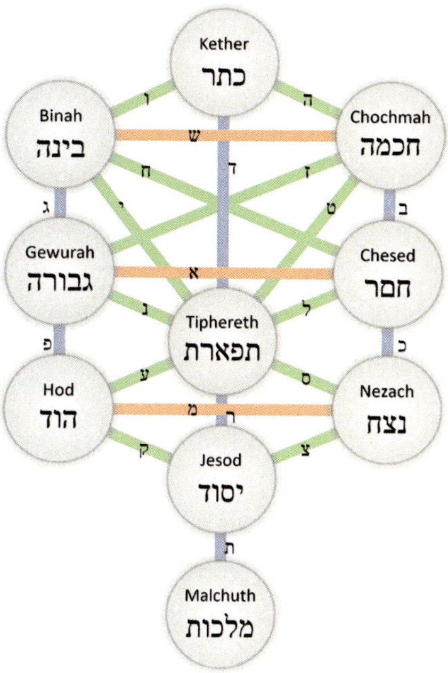

Figure 26. *The Kabbalistic Tree of Life Courtesy of The World Encyclopedia Photo: Johan af Klint*

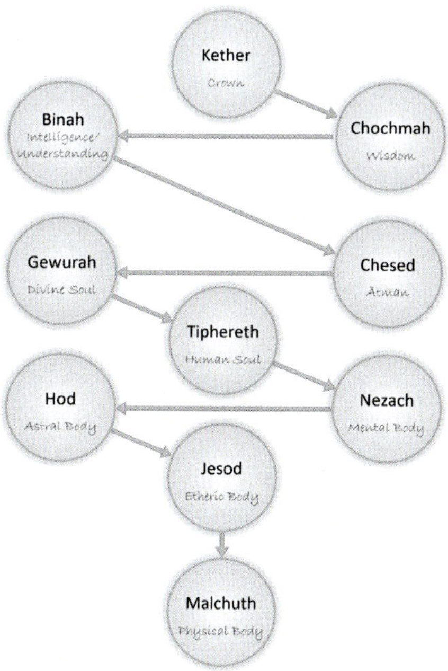

Figure 27. *The Gnostic Kabbalistic Tree of Life Courtesy of Glorian Publishing Photo: Johan af Klint*

What is the Spiritual Message to Humanity Inherent in the *Drawings to the Temple*?

As indicated above, Hilma af Klint's symbolic works were inter alia based on her interest in cartography, natural science, philosophy and religion.

Consequently, based also on our present knowledge of modern natural science, a serious effort has been made to learn what the *spiritual message to humanity* inherent in her *Drawings to the Temple* could mean. The research efforts and analysis are well documented. However, in this article, the presentation is purposely limited to only a few comments on quantum physics, on C. G. Jung's teachings, on Dag Hammarskjöld's view, on Mentalism, and on Hilma af Klint's own views.

Not being a quantum physicist, the author is aware that there may be some weaknesses in the approach below. So far in this article, the various views expressed are based on facts derived from the notebooks of the Hilma af Klint estate. However, regarding this aspect—the attempt to decipher the *spiritual message to humanity* included in the *Drawings to the Temple*, the author's views are based on incontestable facts, as well as to a certain extent on his own views. Having done a serious analysis, it is nevertheless regarded as being worthwhile to suggest an earnest proposal as to what the *spiritual message to humanity* inherent in the *Drawings to the Temple* potentially could constitute. Given this, the author sincerely invites the academic world to review this suggested proposal on an interdisciplinary basis, to criticize it, and to further develop the same.

1. *Quantum Physics*

Quantum physics[150] is the branch of physics that describes the actions of matter and of energy in microcosmos—i.e. on the atomic and sub-atomic levels. At these levels, energy appears in indivisible amounts (*quanta*). In addition, the applicable laws at these levels differ from those of Newton's physics of materialism and of Darwin's biology of survival.

From quantum physics we learn that *our material world is ultimately based on non-material elements.* On a sub-atomic level, the matter is transformed into a world of invisible and non-matter forms, where neither time nor space exists—i.e. the *potentiality*. These non-matter forms constitute together the *cosmic world of potentiality*, from which all empirical aspects derive.[151]

When we observe the particle, it takes the form of a visible matter. When we leave it in isolation, it transforms into a wave. The wave is non-visible—it has no mass, no energy, and no specific location. It assumes only the possibility to be either here or there. *We thus affect the matter, when we observe it.*

150 For further information, please see:

Max Planck's hypothesis about quantification of the beaming from black matters (1900);

Albert Einstein's theoretical explanation of the Photoelectric effect (1905);

Niels Bohr's model of the atom (1913);

Louis Broglie's suggestion that electrons have wave qualities (1924);

Erwin Schrödinger's and Werner Heiselberg's Quantum Mechanics (1925).

151 Schäfer, 2013, pp. xxi, 5, 9 & 19–23.

Eddington, 1929, p. 279.

The entities in the non-material realm of *cosmic potentiality* are not particles—they may be seen as *forms and waves*.[152] Albeit being invisible to us, these *forms and waves* are real, as they can manifest themselves in the empirical world and to have an impact on it.[153]

These forms and waves (i.e. vibrations or "strings" in the String Theory) are non-local and make up the realm of cosmic potentiality. The *cosmic potentiality* may be regarded as an indivisible wholeness—*the One*—in which all living beings and all matters are interconnected.[154] There are indications, that *forms and waves* in the *cosmic potentiality* are *patterns of consciousness-like information—i.e. like the thoughts in our mind.* They do not contain any matter, nor any energy. They just state what is possible in the world.[155] The similarities to the *Ākāśa-Chronicle*[156] and to the Buddhist *Ālāyavijñāna*[157] are striking.

152 Pythagoras (sixth century BCE) stated that "*all things are numbers*" and Plato (fifth century BCE) claimed that atoms were "*mathematical forms.*"

Russel, 1979, p. 54.

The base of our universe is presently intensively studied and disputed among natural scientists.

Professor Max Tegmark (at the MIT) advocates for instance the concept of "*multi-universe*" and also claims that "*our physical world is mathematic.*"

Rose, 2017, pp. 297 ff & 208.

153 Schäfer, 2013, p. 15.

154 Schäfer, 2013, p. 9.

Please note the similarities of this indivisible wholeness—*the One*—with the Buddhist Ultimate Reality—"*All-is-One & One-is-All.*"

155 Ponte & Schäfer, 2013, p. 601.

156 See Footnote 55 above.

157 See Footnote 56 above.

Heisenberg's Uncertainty Principle not only revolutionized atomic physics, but also opened new avenues for exploring the nature of reality, including the possibility of higher dimensional spaces.[158]

To summarize the effects of the quantum physics, one may state that:

> *All empirical aspects are emanations of the realm of cosmic potentiality and are based on consciousness.*

2. *Carl Gustav Jung*

C. G. Jung's (1875–1961) teachings go beyond mere psychology, as they acknowledge *numinous* as the basis of the cosmic order.[159]

C. G. Jung studied the human psyche in such a profound manner that his conclusions transgressed the limitations of the human mind and opened for a *mind*-like background of the universe. He stated:

> *That the world inside and outside ourselves*
> *rests on a transcendent background,*
> *is as certain as our own existence.*[160]

C. G. Jung suggested that our mind is guided by a system of invisible forms, the *archetypes*. They are non-empiric and invisible forms—without any mass or any energy. Nevertheless, the *archetypes* are real and powerful according to C. G. Jung.[161] It may be noted, that Hilma af

158 Villari, 2024, p. 180.

159 Ponte & Schäfer, 2013, p. 602.

160 Jaffé, 1989, p. 30 (Citation of C.G. Jung).

161 Ponte & Schäfer, 2013, p. 601.

Klint also meant that her symbolic works emanated from something that resembles the *archetypes*—the spirits.[162]

These *archetypes* exist according to C. G. Jung in a "*psychic system of a collective, universal and impersonal nature*"[163]—i.e. the *Collective Unconscious.*[164] Note that in recent years, these Jungian concepts have been re-evaluated and deemed not to be preexisting or innate—but (i) according to Knox having emerged from human development[165] or (ii) according to Coleman having emerged from the activity of the symbolic imagination.[166]

We may understand from the above, that the Quantum World—which discovered the realm of non-material *forms and images*—was of great importance to Jung's psychology. The aspect of the cosmic realm made it possible to accept that the *archetypes* do exist and may appear in the *Collective Unconscious.* In this connection, it would be worthwhile to repeat Jung's expression that:

> *It is not only possible, but fairly probable even,*
> *that psyche and matter are two different aspects*
> *of one and the same thing.*[167]

162 HaK 555, pp. 18, 49 & 403, 2 and 4 September 1906 and 4 December 1907.

163 Jung, 1969 [3], pp. 43–44.

164 Jung, 1969 [3], pp. 4 & 43.

165 Knox, 2011, pp. 14–15.

166 Andrigo Moreira, 2020, p. 41.

167 Jung, 1960, p. 418 (which was also presented above in Hilma af Klint's Philosophy of Life—aspect No. VIII).

3. *Dag Hammarskjöld*

The former Secretary General of the United Nations—Dag Hammarskjöld—wrote in his book "*Road Signs*"[168] that:

> *Resting in the center of our beings we meet a world,*
> *where everything is resting in itself.*
> *Hereby, the tree becomes a mystery, the cloud a revelation,*
> *the man a cosmos, the riches of which*
> *we perceive and understand only in glimpses.*[169]

4. *Mentalism*

Mentalism proposes that the "*True Consciousness*" is the *only reality*. It may not be located anywhere—neither in space, nor in time.

The "*World Consciousness*" comes into existence as a "*thought*" inside the True Consciousness. The World Consciousness may be found everywhere—in space, as well as in time. The World Consciousness is a *consciousness, in which everything is an Entity—and this Entity is everything; i.e. "All is One, One is All."*

168 "*Vägmärken*" published in 1963.

169 "*Vilande i vårt väsens centrum möter vi en värld, där allt på samma sätt vilar i sig. Därvid blir trädet ett mysterium, molnet en uppenbarelse, människan ett kosmos vars rikedom vi fattar och förstår endast i glimtar.*"

Hammarskjöld, 1963, p. 141, 4 August 1959.

Our universe has emerged as a "*thought*" within the World Consciousness. Our universe is thus a "*thought within a thought*" and *based on consciousness.*[170]

5. *Hilma af Klint*

Hilma af Klint mentions in her script *Studies of the Life of the Soul* that "*... what is happening in the material world is the same thing that happens in Heaven only with the difference that the former has a firmer form, while the latter is to be considered as a thought form—or more concretely, the thought in Heaven has been realized on earth.*"[171] Please note, that Hilma af Klint herewith assumes the Hermetic theme "As above, so below" and what it entails (See Item IX on page 54 above).

170 Brunton, 2020, pp. 131, 156–157 & 170–175.

A comparison could in this respect also be made with *Platonism* (Plato 427–347 BCE) with its distinction between the world of ideas and the world of senses. A comparison could furthermore be made with *Neoplatonism* (Sakkas and Plotinus during the 3rd Century CE) which states that consciousness encompassses everything and gives it life. It is rather similar to the concept of the Buddhist *Yogācāra-cittamātra*, which states that "*All is Mind.*"

171 "*... vad som försiggår i materiens värld är detsamma som försiggår inom Himmelriket endast med den skillnaden att det ena äger en fastare form, det andra däremot är att betrakta såsom en tankeform, eller rättare uttryckt, tanken inom Himmelriket har blivit realiserad inom jordelivet.*"

HaK 421–HaK 430, p. 665, 11 June 1917.

Conclusion

Based on the above references to quantum physics, to Carl Gustav Jung, to Dag Hammarskjöld, to Mentalism, and to Hilma af Klint, we arrive at the following potential interpretation of the meaning of the *spiritual message to humanity* inherent in Hilma af Klint's symbolic works; viz. that:

> *We are in the process of leaving*
> *Materialism (i.e. Darwin's biology and Newton's physics)*
> *to embrace*
> *Mentalism (where everything is based on consciousness).*

The Afterword

Afterword

Johan af Klint's article, *Hilma af Klint's Philosophy of Life,* offers a deeply insightful and personal exploration of his great aunt's spiritual and artistic legacy. Drawing on his meticulous study of Hilma af Klint's extensive notebooks—spanning over 26,000 pages—Johan presents his interpretation of the spiritual philosophies and artistic intentions that shape her work. These notebooks offer a wealth of information, not only about her creative process but also about the spiritual experiences that informed her symbolic work. Johan's detailed analysis, supported by numerous footnotes, offers a valuable resource for future academic researchers seeking to engage with the deeper layers of meaning within her spiritual message.

In his article, Johan emphasizes his perspective that Hilma af Klint's work was deeply rooted in spiritual traditions including Rosicrucianism, Theosophy and Christianity. From this vantage point, he interprets her *Drawings to the Temple* and other symbolic work as sacred creations to convey a profound "spiritual message to humanity from higher dimensions." This interpretation aligns with Johan's view that her symbolic motifs transcend the artistic sphere, serving as a bridge between ethereal and physical realms. By reconnecting her symbolic work with these religious and philosophical contexts, Johan helps us to better understand af Klint's vision as a synthesis of spiritual and esoteric knowledge.

My own research complements Johan's work in analyzing Hilma af Klint's blending of spiritual and scientific inquiry, particularly in her *Atom* and *Tree of Knowledge* series. Like Johan, I view her work as more than a visual representation; it reflects the interconnectedness of the universe—exploring the duality of material and spiritual dimensions. My studies have focused on how af Klint's integration of esoteric philosophies informed her symbolic language, allowing her to merge metaphysical concepts with scientific paradigms of her time. Her spiritual journey ultimately concluded with Anthroposophy, which later became a cornerstone of her worldview and even influenced the preservation of her work—a sentiment she expressed in a 1943 letter to an acquaintance, cautioning that 'placing it one day in the hands of those who do not share an anthroposophical perspective might be precarious.' Her significant symbolic work, particularly those grounded in spiritism, offer a profound commentary on the quest for truth, extending far beyond the boundaries of art history.

What is particularly striking about Johan's article is how it repositions Hilma af Klint as not merely a forerunner of abstract art but as a mystic and prophet whose work offers a spiritual blueprint for humanity. Through his careful analysis of her *Drawings to the Temple*—the correct translation of the title af Klint herself preferred over the more commonly used "Paintings for the Temple"—Johan reminds us that her work is not simply symbolic but sacred. Johan's familial connection, along with his close collaboration with researchers Hedvig Ersman and Tomas Östlund, gives his perspective a unique authority.

His personal research, much like Hilma af Klint's work, invites us to consider the interwoven relationships between science, spirituality, and philosophy—connections that are often overlooked in traditional art historical discourse. As Johan rightly asserts, Hilma af Klint's legacy is far greater than the label "abstract art" can convey. Her work is intended to be a sacred message, deeply informed by her engagement with spiritual practices and by her contacts with the astral plane. These esoteric influences, combined with her visionary understanding of the universe, have left an indelible mark on the history of art and spirituality. Johan's article contributes meaningfully to our understanding of her philosophies and highlights the need for a more interdisciplinary approach in studying her work—one that integrates spiritual, philosophical, and scientific perspectives, including areas such as quantum physics, which also aligns with my research.

In closing, Johan af Klint's article is not only a profound academic and personal exploration but also a continuation of Hilma af Klint's spiritual mission. Through his insightful analysis, Johan illuminates the sacred nature of her work, emphasizing that her symbolic visual language transcends the confines of time and space to convey a spiritual message to humanity. He helps us recognize the deep interconnectedness between her artistic and spiritual practices, inviting us to consider the broader implications of her vision. As we continue to study her work, it is crucial to remember the spiritual and esoteric foundations that shaped it—foundations that Johan has masterfully uncovered. His article serves as both a valuable resource for scholars and a reminder of the need for a more interdisciplinary approach to understanding af Klint's legacy, one that integrates spiritual, philosophical, and scientific perspectives, including the emerging relevance of quantum physics in her work as a medium and symbolist.

List of Figures

Figure 10. The WUS/Seven-Pointed Star Series, Group VI, *The Evolution, No. 14.* 1908. HaK 082. 1908. 99.5 x 129.5 cm. Oil on canvas.

Figure 11. Comparison of Thomas Young (1773-1829), *A Course on Lectures on Natural Philosophy and the Mechanical Arts, Volume 2, Plates, Figure 450 (1807)* and The SUW Series, Group IX, *The Swan, No. 17.* 1915. HaK 165. 150.5 x 151.0 cm. Oil on canvas.

Figure 12.* The SUW Series, Group IX, *The Swan, No. 23.* 1915. HaK 171. 152.5 x 150.0 cm. Oil on canvas.

Figure 13.* The UW Series, Group IX, *The Dove, No. 3.* 1915. HaK 175. 155.5 x 115.5 cm. Oil on canvas.

Figure 14. *The Atom Series, No. 10.* 1917. HaK 362. 27.0 x 25.0 cm. Watercolor, graphite and metallic paint on paper.

Figure 15.* *The Nordic Nature Studies, Series III, Violet Flowers with Guidelines.* 1919. HaK 457. 50.0 x 27.0 cm. Watercolor, graphite, ink and metallic paint on paper.

Figure 16. Untitled. 1932. HaK 882. 43.0 x 57.0 cm. Watercolor on paper.

Figure 17. The WU/Rose Series, Group I, *Primordial Chaos, No. 1.* 1906. HaK 001. 53.0 x 37.0 cm. Oil on canvas.

Figure 18. *The Atom Series, No. 2.* 1917. HaK 354. 27.0 x 25.0 cm. Watercolor, graphite and metallic paint on paper.

Figure 19.* The *Parsifal* series, *Group II, The Ether Convolute, No. 60.* 1916. HaK 269. 27.0 x 25.0 cm. Watercolor and graphite on paper.

Figure 20. On the Viewing of Flowers and Trees, *Wheat and Wormwood.* 1922. HaK 627. 18.0 x 25.0 cm. Watercolor and graphite on paper.

Note on asterisks *

There are minor variations in the contemporary titles and other identifying information of some of the illustrations. This is due to matters of translation, provenance of the illustrations, multiple renditions of the same illustration by Hilma af Klint, and references to the titles in various published and unpublished works. In most instances the titles presented in the List of Figures and in the pages of the book are based on the most comprehensive reference work, *The Catalogue Raisonné* (7 vol.). The titles of Figures with an asterisk are provided by the author based on his research of published and unpublished sources.

List of Literature

af Klint, Hilma, 1917–1918, "*Studie av Själslivet*," HaK 421–HaK 430, Stockholm, Sweden.

________. Hilma af Klint's letter to Tyra Kleen of 3 September 1943, lodged in the Tyra Kleen archives at the Valinge Farm, Södermanlands Län, Sweden.

Almqvist, Kurt and Daniel Brimbaum, eds. 2020–2022. *The Catalogue Raisonné*, 7 Vol. Bokförlaget Stolpe AB, Stockholm, Sweden.

Andrigo Moreira de Ulhoa Coelho, Mônica, 2020, *Images of Souls—An encounter between Hilma af Klint and Carl G. Jung*, Sao Paulo, Brazil.

Bauduin, Tessel M., 2018, "*Science and Occultism in Hilma af Klint's Time and in her Work*," in the "Hilma af Klint: Paintings for the Future" exhibition catalogue, the Solomon R. Guggenheim Museum, New York, USA, pp. 186–191.

Bashkoff, Tracey, 2024, "*Introducción*" in the "Hilma af Klint" exhibition catalogue, the Guggenheim-Bilbao Museum, Bilbao, Spain, pp. 14–25.

Brunton, Paul, 2020, "*Själens Visdom*," Bokförlaget Robert Larson AB, Stockholm, Sweden.

Burgin, Christine, 2018, *Hilma af Klint—Notes and Methods*, The University of Chicago Press, Chicago, USA.

du Prel, Carl, repr. 2023, *The Philosophy of Mysticism*, Vol. 1 & 2 (1889), Lushana Books.

_______. 1890, *Själsläran—framställd ur Synpunkten af Menniskoväsendets Enhet*, Looström & Komp:s Förlag, Stockholm, Sweden.

________. 1890, *Det Dolda Själslifvet—eller Mystikens Filosofi,* Oscar L. Lamms Förlag, Stockholm, Sweden.

Eddington, Arthur, S., 1929, *The Nature of the Physical World,* MacMillan, New York, USA.

Eidem, Karl, 2024, "*Spinozas resa,*" Unpublished.

Fant, Åke, 1989, *Hilma af Klint, Ockult målarinna och abstrakt pionjär,* Raster Förlag, Stockholm, Sweden.

Glorian, 2024, "*Gnostic Kabbalah: Introduction,*" Glorian Publishing. https://www.glorian.org/Kabbalah/.

HaK The signum in front of the number of each of Hilma af Klint's symbolic works.

Hammarskjöld, Dag, 1963, *Vägmärken,* Albert Bonnier Förlag, Stockholm, Sweden.

Heiser, James D., 2011, *Prisci Theologi and the Hermetic Reformation in the Fifteenth Century,* Malone, Texas, USA.

Henderson, Linda Dalrymple, 2023, "*The Etherial Worldview of the Early Twentieth Century,*" in the "Hilma af Klint & Piet Mondrian: Forms of Life" exhibition catalogue, the Tate Modern Museum, London, England, pp. 170–173.

________. 2019, "*The invisible in Hilma af Klint's occult and scientific context,*" in "Hilma af Klint—Tidsandans Visionär," The Axel and Margaret Ax:son Johnson Foundation, Stockholm, Sweden, pp. 71–91.

Horowitz, David Max, 2024, "*Pinturas para el Museo: Hilma af Klint y el Arte Moderna,*" in the "Hilma af Klint" exhibition catalogue, the Guggenheim-Bilbao Museum, Bilbao, Spain, pp. 34–45.

Høgsberg, Milena & Rudbøg, Tim, 2020, "*Hilma af Klint, the Theosophy, the higher levels of consciousness and the invisible universe*" in the Moderna Museet exhibition catalogue 410, the Moderna Museet Malmö, Sweden, pp. 81–90.

Jaffé, A., 1989, "*Was C.G. Jung a Mystic? And Other Essays,*" the Daimon Verlag, Einsiedeln, Switzerland [Google Scholar].

Jung, C.G., 1969, *The Archetypes and the Collective Unconscious*, Vol. 9, Princeton University Press, Princeton, New Jersey, USA, Collected Works.

Jung, C.G., 1960, *The Structure and Dynamics of the Psyche*, Vol. 8, the Princeton University Press, Princeton, USA, Collected Works.

Kerstein, Benjamin, "Kabbalah," *World History Encyclopedia*, (last modified September 27, 2018) https://www.worldhistory.org/Kabbalah/.

Knox, Jean, 2011, *Self-agency in psychotherapy—attachment, autonomy and intimacy*, the W. W. Norton & Co, New York, USA.

Lundgren, Britt, 2024, "*Action at a Distance: Did physicist Thomas Young's 1807 Lectures inspire some of the earliest examples of abstract art?*" (Has been published in the *Leonardo Journal*, the MIT Press Journals, USA).

Martin (Ahlén), Hedvig, 2018, "*Hilma af Klint och De Fem—Förberedelsetiden 1896–1907*" ("*Hilma af Klint and The Five—The Preparatory Period 1896–1907*"), Master's Thesis, the Institution of History, Södertörns Högskola, Sweden.

McNab, Janice, 2024, *Gallaxy Ballroom—A Dance with Hilma af Klint*, Jap Sam Books, Prinsenbeek, the Netherlands.

Müller-Westermann, Iris, 2020, "*Hilma af Klint—Artist, Researcher, Medium*" in the Moderna Museet exhibition catalogue 410, the Moderna Museet Malmö, Sweden, pp. 25–42.

Pasi, Marco, 2015, "*Hilma af Klint, Western Esotericism and the problem of Modern Artistic Creativity,*" in the "Hilma af Klint—The Art of Seeing the Invisible," the Axel and Margaret Ax:son Johnson Foundation, Stockholm, Sweden, pp. 101–116.

Ponte, Diogo Valadas & Schäfer, Lothar, 2013, "*Carl Gustav Jung, Quantum Physics and the Spiritual Mind: A mystical Vision of the Twenty-First Century,*" The Multidisciplinary Digital Publishing Institute

(MDPI), Behavioral Sciences, Basel, Switzerland, December 2013, 3(4): 601–618.

Rose, Joanna, 2017, *Kosmiskt Pussel—Försöken att förstå universum,* Volante, Stockholm, Sweden.

Russel, B., 1979 (1946), *History of Western Philosophy,* London University, London, England.

Say, Aliya, 2022, "*Art, Spirit and Plant—On Botanical Abstraction, Vegetal Ontology and Mystical States,*" PhD Dissertation, School of Communication and Culture, Department of Art History, Aarhus University, Denmark.

Schäfer, Lothar, 2013, *Infinite Potential—What Quantum Physics Reveals About How We Should Live,* the Deepak Chopra Books, Random House, Inc., New York, USA.

Tate Modern, 2023, in the "*Hilma af Klint and Piet Mondrian: Forms of Life*" exhibition catalogue and in the exhibition guide, # 10, Tate Modern Museum, London, England.

Villari, Rachel, 2024, "*Transcending Dichotomies: Hilma af Klint's confluence of Science and Spiritualism in Atom and the Tree of Knowledge,*" PhD Dissertation, Salve Regina University, Newport, Rhode Island, USA.

Voss, Julia, 2024, "*In the name of the Snail—The utopia of Hilma af Klint,*" in the "Hilma af Klint" exhibition catalogue, the Guggenheim-Bilbao Museum, Bilbao, Spain, pp. 46–57.

________. 2022, *Hilma af Klint—A Biography,* The University of Chicago Press, Chicago, USA.

________. 2018, "*The Traveling Hilma af Klint,*" in the "Hilma af Klint: Paintings for the Future" exhibition catalogue, the Solomon R Guggenheim Museum, New York, USA, pp. 48–63.

Acknowledgements

The author would like to take this opportunity of presenting his acknowledgement to Hedvig Ersman and to Tomas Östlund, with whom he has worked closely regarding the research of Hilma af Klint and her symbolic works. They have both been of valuable assistance to me in the research for this article.

The author would also like to extend his appreciation to Timothy J. Demy, who has been very kind, to ensure that this Monograph has been printed and published. He has been of importance in having the views of Hilma af Klint and of her symbolic works corrected and rectified—for the benefit of future academic researchers.

The author would also like to extend his gratitude to Rachel Villari, whose PhD dissertation from 2024 reflects the interconnectedness of the universe—embracing both the material and the spiritual aspects. Rachel Villari has kindly edited this article and has hereby proposed valuable information. She has also been so kind as to write the Afterword.

About the Author and Editor

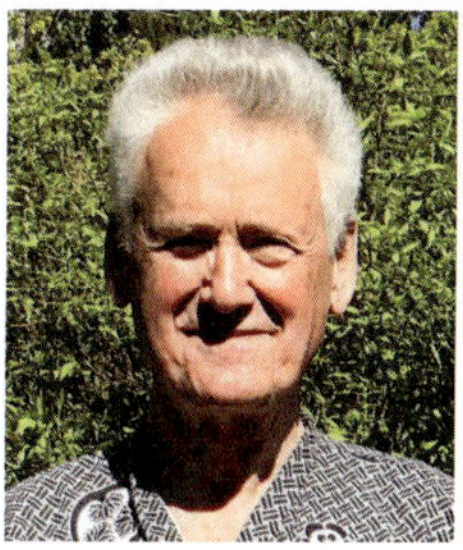

Johan af Klint (1939) has a PhD in religious history with concentration on Buddhism at the Stockholm University (2021). His professional education encompasses the Civilekonom examination at the Stockholm School of Economics, a MA examination at the Stockholm University and a MBA at the University of California, Berkeley.

Johan af Klint has worked in finance in the Far East, in Europe, in the USA and in Sweden. He was involved in the establishment of the Asian Development Bank in Manilla and in a new merchant bank in London, as well as in the reoganization of the Svenska Handelsbanken unit in New York. He has also established and ran the financial departments of the LM Ericsson Group and of the Svenska Petroleum AB. Finally, he has established and ran one of the first Venture Capital companies in Sweden.

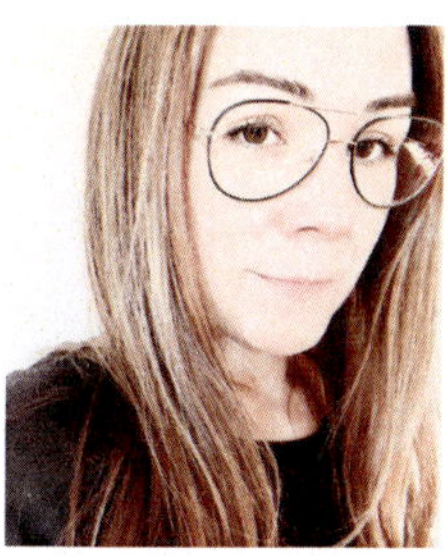

Rachel Villari, PhD, is an artist, professor, and art historian specializing in the life and work of Hilma af Klint. Her research, as outlined in her dissertation *Transcending Dichotomies: Hilma af Klint's Confluence of Science and Spiritualism in Atom and the Tree of Knowledge*, examines the symbolic visual language in af Klint's work and its connections to the intersections of art, science, and spiritualism. As a scholar, she is committed to amplifying the contributions of historically overlooked artists, particularly women whose voices have been marginalized in art history. By combining studio practice and art historical analysis, her work highlights af Klint's innovative approaches and their broader cultural significance. She explores the greater significance and meaning in af Klint's work and is dedicated to helping protect and safeguard her legacy.